What people are saying about …

GLORIOUS RUIN

"*Glorious Ruin* is a transforming reminder not to run from our suffering, but to learn from it! Tullian Tchividjian courageously opens up his life to share how God didn't save him from pain, but met him in the middle of his suffering. At some point we all face suffering, and this book will not only teach you how to get through it, but will help you discover how it can set you free!"

Dave Ferguson, lead pastor of
Community Christian Church and
movement leader of NewThing

"As a pastor and as a man who has sat under immense difficulty I couldn't be more pleased and excited about what Tullian has done here. This is a book on suffering with the rare combination of truth and compassion, honesty and empathy. Suffering is a reality at some level for all of us, and whether you are currently in a storm or need to understand what our great God and King is accomplishing in and through suffering, this book will serve you well. Biblically saturated and faithful, *Glorious Ruin* is a gift to the hurting, confused, and curious and will prepare many to marvel at the goodness and grace of God in all circumstances."

Matt Chandler, lead pastor of The
Village Church and president of
Acts 29 Church Planting Network

"Having lived with quadriplegia for over forty-five years, I know how critical it is to think 'rightly' about suffering—indeed, the jaws of pain will rip your faith to shreds if you don't have a solid view of what Scripture has to say on the subject. It's why I applaud men of God like Tullian—men who've dug deep into God's Word to help us grasp the mysterious connection between Christ, His cross, and the crucible of our afflictions. That's what makes *Glorious Ruin* a blessing!"

Joni Eareckson Tada, Joni and Friends International Disability Center

"*Glorious Ruin* is set apart by its depth of human understanding—the pastoral facts-on-the-ground of how people actually experience suffering—and by its depth of appropriation of the deepest Christian resources for helping people in their suffering. Tullian unmasks the unhelpful diagnoses that the world and the church often offer sufferers. But then Tullian offers a way forward! It is a deep and wide way, built upon the cross of Christ. There is another absolutely terrific thing about this book: it is filled to the brim with memorable stories and quotations. *Glorious Ruin* is a treasure chest from the 'red cross,' designed perfectly for persons living in the midst of pain."

Paul F. M. Zahl, author of *Grace in Practice*

"Tullian Tchividjian's *Glorious Ruin* is a gospel-driven tour de force. This book comes at you like a torrent of rain on a hot day—if you're suffering or feeling that dull kind of pain we all feel in our lives from time to time, you must read *Glorious Ruin*. Tullian shows how no matter what you're going through, God stands with you in your suffering and is everything you'll ever need. I couldn't recommend this book more highly!"

Mark Batterson, lead pastor of National Community Church, Washington, DC, and *New York Times* best-selling author of *The Circle Maker*

"Nothing is as certain for your life and mine as suffering—and eventual death. Heartache and pain come in all sorts of packages. So the only mature thing to do is to prepare for it. In a culture that seems pathologically upbeat, living in the moment and in denial of any blue notes, the message of this book desperately needs to be heard far and wide. Read it while you can."

Michael Horton, professor of theology and apologetics at Westminster Seminary California and president of The White Horse Inn

"*Glorious Ruin* is a powerful, vulnerable, and gospel-centered work. I love Tullian's heart for comforting those who are hurting, broken, or suffering in our world. And in this book he shows how God is constantly present with us. Always. No matter what your circumstances."

Brad Lomenick, executive director of Catalyst

"Into our culture of mandatory happiness, Tullian Tchividjian speaks a deeply sensitive, thoroughly cross-centered theology of suffering that far surpasses the typical pabulum offered by theologians of glory: 'Your suffering isn't so bad! What doesn't make you bitter will make you better! You're suffering because you don't have enough faith!' There were no pat answers for Job, and there are none here either (thank God!). Let me encourage you to dive into this book and the suffering that's drawing you to it simply because 'our hope does not lie in this temporal life; it lies in the life to come.'"

Elyse Fitzpatrick, conference speaker
and author of *Give Them Grace*

"Nothing gets our attention more than suffering. In *Glorious Ruin*, Tullian helps us respond rightly to God in the midst of our struggle. He helps us move from mere desperation to get out of pain, to trust in God through the pain. I highly recommend this book for the nitty-gritty of real life."

Darrin Patrick, pastor of The Journey and
author of *Church Planter* and *For the City*

"Tullian's fresh approach to suffering is theologically rich, pastorally sensitive, and prophetically challenging. He has redirected the pain of suffering from the one suffering to where it belongs—the God who was crucified on our behalf. Suffering can only be understood through the lens of Calvary. Thank you, Tullian, for yet another Christ-centered book!"

Preston M. Sprinkle, associate
professor of Eternity Bible College

"Like you, I'm a sufferer. For the last three years I have watched my eight-year-old daughter suffer with cancer. As I write this, there is a very good chance that she won't be around when you read it. This book helped me face that hard reality. The Why and How of suffering have been of little value to my family and me over the last few years. The truth of the Who and grace, so wonderfully presented in this book, has been our life and only hope. Thank you, Tullian, for both your insight and honesty. Reader, enjoy Jesus and grace as you suffer—they're there."

Britt Merrick, founder of the Reality family of churches, pastor for preaching and vision at Reality Santa Barbara, author of *Godspeed* and *Big God*

"The question of suffering is the apologetic question of our time. From both Christians and non-Christians alike it is the question I get most often. *Glorious Ruin* reminds us that pain and suffering are a part of not only human existence but also the Christian experience. Tullian has written a wonderfully helpful book on how to suffer well, facing its reality and being hopeful of its reward."

Dave Lomas, lead pastor of Reality San Francisco

"It is true that between the 'already' and the 'not yet,' suffering is the inescapable, universal human experience. But when you suffer, you don't just suffer what you are suffering, you suffer the way you are suffering. It is here that my friend Tullian makes his greatest contribution. In exposing our tendency to greet our suffering with self-righteous legalism and denial, he leaves us in our moment of pain with only one place to run, hide, and rest. No, we are not counseled here to run to the hope that we will increasingly learn suffering's lessons and suffer more nobly. Rather, we are faced with the mess that we all are, and we are again and again reminded of the grace of the Savior who perfectly suffered on our behalf. It is this grace alone that frees us from the burden of suffering being the place where we are called to prove our faith to ourselves, to others, and to God, and allows us in doubt, anger, fear, and dismay to run into the arms of our tender, patient, kind, and gracious Suffering Savior."

Paul Tripp, counselor and author
of *What Did You Expect?*

GLORIOUS RUIN

TULLIAN TCHIVIDJIAN

GLORIOUS RUIN

how
suffering
sets
you
free

GLORIOUS RUIN
Published by David C Cook
4050 Lee Vance View
Colorado Springs, CO 80918 U.S.A.

David C Cook Distribution Canada
55 Woodslee Avenue, Paris, Ontario, Canada N3L 3E5

David C Cook U.K., Kingsway Communications
Eastbourne, East Sussex BN23 6NT, England

LCCN 2012944300
ISBN 978-1-4347-0402-3
eISBN 978-1-4347-0515-0

Published in association with Yates & Yates, www.yates2.com.

The Team: Alex Field, Nick Lee, Renada Arens, Karen Athen
Cover Design: Amy Konyndyk
Cover Photo: Veer

Printed in the United States of America
First Edition 2012

1 2 3 4 5 6 7 8 9 10

071712

TABLE OF CONTENTS

ACKNOWLEDGMENTS

This book started out as a series of sermons I preached through the book of Job following a very painful season of life. Apparently they struck a chord because they quickly became the most-listened-to sermons I've ever preached. I heard from people all over the world who told me how God had used these sermons to set them free from the bitterness, anger, and despair that always accompany seasons of ache. Their testimonies alone compelled me to write this book.

But this book is not the sermons. Well, it would be more accurate to say that this book is much, much more than the sermons. And for that, I have a few people I really want to thank.

My good friend Justin Holcomb took the transcriptions and, along with Matt Johnson, provided the structure, the flow, and a working manuscript. It's not an easy thing to go through hundreds of pages of transcribed sermons and structure a book. Justin and his team are second to none.

And then my much-admired friend David Zahl went to work. David's literary skill, cultural insight, and theological profundity are a lethal combination. He filled in the gaps, provided the polish, and made this book what it is from beginning to end. He is a writer/editor of the highest rank. I thank God for your gifts, David. But even more so for your friendship.

I also want to thank my agent, Sealy Yates, who believes in what God has compelled me to say and wants to do everything he can to help me say it.

And finally, I want to thank all of my friends at David C Cook, especially Alex Field, for your partnership. You guys are amazing. You really are. Your enthusiasm for what I want to say is so refreshing and encouraging. You're a privilege to work with.

INTRODUCTION

There is a temptation in writing a book about suffering to romanticize one's struggles or, worse, to insensitively rank and compare trials, as if victimhood were a matter of one-upmanship. Far too many people have suffered the sort of tragic reversals that I have been spared, and no one but God knows or understands the full extent of another person's pain. At the same time, people who haven't experienced major setbacks sometimes feel that their hurts are somehow less legitimate or real. The English poet T. S. Eliot once wrote, "All cases are unique, and very similar to others,"[1] and I think he was on to something. Suffering is suffering, and it is universal. The sincere hope of this short book is to explore how the reality of human suffering, in all its forms, might relate to the truth of God's liberating grace in a way that is both honest and comforting.

There are only a few guarantees in life, and unfortunately, the R.E.M. song "Everybody Hurts" articulates one of the most pronounced. We all suffer. Pain is unavoidable, and it's not a question of *if* but *when*. It can take the form of a sudden catastrophe such as the news of a brain tumor or an oncoming hurricane, or it can be something more ordinary like a strained relationship that never seems to get easier, dragging on in a kind of dull ache. There are physical sources of suffering, of course, and there are emotional sources; sometimes they are one and the same. Sometimes the source is obvious and sometimes it is hidden, such as the slow-boiling anxiety or depression that haunts us even in our happiest moments. In fact, for some of us, pain has become such a pervasive fact of daily life that we've grown numb to it. Others feel it more acutely, doing whatever they can to alleviate the feeling by means of self-medication. Whatever your experience, whatever variety of pain you're most familiar with, the truth remains: each of us suffers in some way, every single day.

Sadly, the ways in which we cope with pain, loss, and tragedy often make the problems worse. Perhaps we roll up our sleeves and get down to the business of fixing things (and people!). Or perhaps we succumb to the can-do, Pollyanna optimism of our surrounding culture, put on a happy face, and try to think positive. If only our churches were immune to such approaches!

Have you ever felt like you couldn't share the details of a difficult situation without someone immediately offering a solution or a spiritual platitude? Have you ever responded that way yourself? The required cheerfulness that characterizes many of our churches produces a suffocating environment of pat, religious answers to the painful, complex questions that riddle the lives of hurting people. We will look at how this culture of mandatory happiness actually promotes dishonesty and more suffering.

Why then do we suffer? Why does God allow so much of it? What, if anything, are we supposed to learn through it? And, most importantly, when will it end? Nothing forces us to confront the deeper questions of life quite like suffering. Nothing makes us face the gnawing emptiness inside more nakedly. Nothing confirms our suspicion more powerfully that this is *not* how things are supposed to be.

Naturally, philosophers and theologians have wrestled with the implications of suffering throughout the ages. They have asked, as we do, what suffering means, what it says about human beings and reality in general. In my book *Jesus + Nothing = Everything*, I touched at some length on the *everything*-ness inside every man and woman that begs to be met, the ravenous appetite that we all seek to fill, often via destructive and self-destructive behavior. In the fourth century, Augustine of Hippo captured this internal void in his *Confessions* by wisely observing, "You have made us for Yourself, and our hearts are restless until they find their rest in You."[2] Twelve centuries later, French thinker Blaise Pascal asked, "What is it then … which [man] in vain tries to fill from all his surroundings, seeking from things absent the help he does not obtain in things present? But these are all inadequate, because the infinite abyss can only be filled by an infinite and immutable Object, that is to say, only by God Himself."[3] Later still, that inimitable English professor C. S. Lewis wrote, "If I find in myself a desire which no experience in this world can satisfy, the most probable explanation is that I was made for another world."[4] In other words, this side of heaven, suffering often points to a deeper reality, an indicator of both personal and cosmic discord.

We are meant for something greater. Something far less painful.

Of course, understanding the root and inevitability of pain is rarely enough to alleviate or reduce it. The Nobel Prize–winning social psychologist Daniel Kahneman has built a storied career proving the limits of self-knowledge when it comes to suffering. Even when we know where the hurt is coming from, we tend to respond in one of two ways: we *moralize* or we *minimize*.

Moralists interpret misfortune as the karmic result of misbehavior. This for that. "You failed to obey God, so He gave your child an illness." Such rule-based economies of punishment and reward may be the default mode of the fallen human heart, but that doesn't make them any less brutal! This does not mean that sin doesn't have consequences. If you blow all of your money on booze, you will likely reap poverty, loneliness, and cirrhosis of the liver. Simple cause and effect. But to conclude that suffering people have somehow heaped up trouble for themselves on the Cosmic Registry and that God is doling out the misery in direct proportion would be more than mistaken; it would be cruel. The humorist Jack Handey perceptively parodied such ideas in his *Saturday Night Live*–featured book *Deep Thoughts*:

> If a kid asks where rain comes from, I think a cute thing to tell him is "God is crying." And if he asks

> why God is crying, another cute thing to tell him is, "Probably because of something you did."[5]

The second and equally counterproductive impulse when it comes to suffering is the one that minimizes. Have you ever heard someone try to comfort a grieving friend, saying, "Death is a natural part of life"? The intention may be compassionate, but the recipient seldom experiences it that way. For them, you have just minimized their pain, implying that death and devastation are morally neutral, that our perceptions are what ultimately create the problem of pain—that if we were only able to detach from our emotions, we would experience peace in life, no matter the circumstances. And while there is a certain truth to that—Paul does ask, "Death, where is thy sting?" (1 Cor. 15:55 KJV)—in the moment, it can convey immense insensitivity. Moreover, we minimize suffering when we instrumentalize it. That is, when we subordinate suffering to the result it might achieve, or when we reduce it to a glorified means of self-improvement, as certain daytime talk show hosts might be accused of doing. Christians, of course, use spiritual language to minimize suffering constantly, even their own. The need to exonerate God in the midst of tragedy—even to shove Bible verses in a person's face (regardless of how profound or true they may be)—can be just as harmful as saying something actively discouraging, as if God were small enough to be invalidated by our individual suffering.

Both the moralizing and the minimizing approaches are attempts to keep suffering at bay, to play God. It is safe to say that when our faith (or lack thereof) feels like a fight *against* the realities of suffering instead of a resource for *accepting* them, we are on the wrong track. Writer and theologian Robert Farrar Capon has suggested that perhaps we need to "turn the question around—the message is *for* suffering and conflicted people. Christ on the cross meets us *in* our suffering and conflicts not in the promise to take them away. He is simply *with* us in all our times" (emphasis original).[6] Capon means that our hope is not "Jesus plus an explanation as to why suffering happens," or "Jesus plus an explanation as to why you have this job, that spouse, or these circumstances or pain." He is suggesting that God is especially present in suffering. As we will discover, this is the foundation of what is known as the "theology of the cross," as opposed to a "theology of glory," which sees God as present in victory rather than defeat. This is an absolutely crucial distinction, and one that we will unpack at length in the first chapter.

Any discussion of suffering, be it theological, philosophical, or literary, must reckon with the book of Job. His story stands not only as the most prominent and extended meditation on the subject in the Bible but the most iconic one in the entire Western canon. The book of Job tells the story of a wealthy, righteous man who had seven sons and three daughters. In the prologue, Satan asserted that Job was faithful only because God had put a "wall around" him and "blessed" him with prosperity. If God took everything Job had, then he would surely curse the heavens. God gave Satan permission to test Job's righteousness.

All of Job's possessions were destroyed; his vast stores of livestock stolen or burned up by "the fire of God [that] fell from the sky" (Job 1:16), and a mighty wind tragically wiped out all of Job's children. Yet Job did not curse God. Instead he shaved his head, tore his clothes, and uttered those famous words: "Naked I came from my mother's womb, and naked shall I return. The LORD gave, and the LORD has taken away; blessed be the name of LORD" (Job 1:21 ESV).

After Job endured these travesties without reproaching God, Satan sought permission to afflict his person as well, and God consented, so long as Job's life would be spared. Satan then infected him with agonizing boils, leading Job to scrape his skin with broken pottery. His wife responded by telling him to "curse God and die" (2:9 ESV). Next, the unfashionably named trio of Eliphaz, Bildad, and Zophar came to console him, spending a full seven days, sitting on the ground with their miserable friend without saying a word. At last, Job broke his silence and "cursed the day of his birth" (3:1 ESV) at which point the four men engaged in a lengthy (and unhelpful) discussion of Job's plight, which constitutes the majority of the book.

Their discourse illustrates the fundamental moralizing and minimizing tendencies of the human heart, not to mention the spiritual dynamics of blame. Ultimately, however, we will find that the book of Job gives us a clearer understanding of who God is—*and isn't*—in the midst of suffering.

So what would a God who was present in suffering look like? First and foremost, He would be a God who suffers Himself.

Maybe even dies. A God who meets people in their suffering, rather than on the other side of it. Pain might even be one of His primary avenues for reaching people. C. S. Lewis memorably captured this reality when he described pain as God's "megaphone to rouse a deaf world."[7] Southern writer Flannery O'Connor expressed the same truth this way:

> Violence is strangely capable of returning my characters to reality and preparing them to accept their moment of grace. Their heads are so hard that almost nothing else will do the work. This idea, that reality is something to which we must be returned at considerable cost, is one which is seldom understood by the casual reader, but it is one which is implicit in the Christian view of the world.[8]

The description has rung true in my own life.

I'll never forget where I was when I got the call. We were on I-95, heading south. After two years of living in Knoxville, Tennessee, my family and I were returning home to southern Florida to plant a church, and we were excited. It was not going to be easy, but it was going to be a lot easier *there* than it would be anywhere else. You see, in my hometown I was more than an anonymous pastor. I was a *Tchividjian*. My parents were well established in the community; my mother as a nationally renowned speaker and author, the daughter of Billy Graham;

my father a sophisticated European psychologist whose practice helped countless people in the area, not to mention the country. My pedigree would be a huge boost. So when I heard my father's voice on the line, telling me that he and my mother were separating after forty-one years of marriage, I didn't know what to say. Little did I know that it was just the beginning of a painful journey that would turn my life and faith upside down.

My parents' divorce is simply one particularly poignant example. In fact, I have experienced God using painful events to wake me up and free me of unbelief and idolatry more times than I would care to admit. In the case of my parents, I had told myself that as long as I was their son, *I was someone*. So when they announced their separation, it flipped my world upside down. I began to question everything: who I was, what I'd been taught, even the validity of their faith. It was almost like the movie *The Sixth Sense*; I had to go back and reinterpret my entire life through the lens of recent events. It was painful. Indeed, it is always painful when our idols crumble and fall apart, as they inevitably do.

Idols are much more than statues that our ancestors bowed down to. Anything that we build our lives on, anything that we lean on for meaning or identity, anything that we hope will bring us freedom, can be an idol. One of my idols at that point in my life was my family's reputation and the stability of my parents' marriage and faith. The grief brought me to my knees, and put me in touch with my need for God in a way that nothing else could have at that moment.

Yet prayer and repentance were not my immediate response. Stubborn sinner that I am, it took a little while to get there. Whenever what we've depended on for meaning—and it's usually one of God's good gifts—is stripped away, our first reaction tends to be one of anger, self-pity, blame, and entitlement. But idolatry feeds on itself, robbing us of joy until we have no other choice but to cry out for God. Fortunately, as one friend puts it, God's office is at the end your rope.

Indeed, God intends to free us from more than our idolatry; He intends to free us from ourselves. He even wants to liberate us from our need to find a silver lining in suffering. We see this powerful truth play out in the life of Job. His wife rebuked him, his friends condemned him, and his family deserted him. Job lost everything. He could not fix what happened to him, much less stop or explain it. In fact, he could barely hold on. Thankfully, the good news of the gospel is *not* an exhortation from above to "hang on at all costs," or "grin and bear it" in the midst of hardship. No, the good news is that God is hanging on to *you*, and in the end, when all is said and done, the power of God will triumph over every pain and loss. William James once wrote, "Where [God] is, tragedy is only provisional and partial, and shipwreck and dissolution are not the absolutely final things."[9]

So why write another book on suffering?

Certainly we have enough works on the topic already, books that attempt to explain why God allows suffering, presumably in a way that ultimately lets God off the hook. And while much smarter people than me have constructed elaborate systems in this pursuit—the fancy word for such a theory is *theodicy*—they are by definition exercises in speculation. To know the Why would be to grasp the mind of God, which is something none of us can do.

We have enough books tackling the How. How suffering can and will transform our lives, how we can leverage pain and tragedy to make us better people. Results, results, results! Underneath this hopeful veneer, such philosophies tend to fall flat when things don't go according to plan, when we find out that our power, especially in the face of suffering, is a lot more limited than we thought. Pain would not be pain if we could harness it for personal gain, though the tendency to attempt to do so is a universal one. Thankfully, this is not one of those philosophies either. This is not to say that How and Why are not honest questions. Of course they are! And we will explore a few common attempts to answer them. But How and Why can also be a prison. They can leave us cold and confused, just as they left Job cold and confused when his friends tried to formulate their own tedious answers. Information is seldom enough to heal a wounded heart. The question I would like to emphasize instead—and the only one that will ultimately point us toward the truth—is the *Who* amid our suffering. Which is fortunate, since it is the only question that God has seen fit to answer, concretely, in the person and work of Jesus Christ.

> Answers to prayers for help are a problem only when you look on God as a divine vending machine programmed to dispense Cokes, Camels,

> lost keys, and freedom from gall-bladder trouble to anyone who has the right coins. With the personal analogy, things are better.... It isn't that [God] has a principle about not starting cars—or about starting them. What he has a principle about is *you*.... He loves you; his chief concern is to *be himself for you*. (emphasis original)[10]

Do you see it? We may not ever fully understand why God allows the suffering that devastates our lives. We may not ever find the right answers to how we'll dig ourselves out. There may not be any silver lining, especially not in the ways we would like. But we don't need answers as much as we need God's presence in and through the suffering itself. For the life of the believer, one thing is beautifully and abundantly true: God's chief concern in your suffering is to be *with* you and be Himself *for* you.

In other words, our ruin may not ultimately spell our undoing. It may in fact spell the beginning of faith. And in the end, that is enough. *Gloriously so.*

NOTES

1. T. S. Eliot, *The Cocktail Party*, act 2, scene 1 (New York: Mariner Books, 1964).
2. Augustine, *Confessions*, I, 1.
3. Blaise Pascal, *Pensées*, section VII, 425.
4. C. S. Lewis, *Mere Christianity* (New York: Macmillan, 1952), 120.

5. Jack Handey, *Deep Thoughts: Inspiration for the Uninspired* (New York: Berkley Books, 1992), 3.
6. Robert Farrar Capon, "The Outrageousness of God's Indiscriminating Grace: Mockingbird Interviews Robert Farrar Capon," *Mockingbird*, September 2, 2011, accessed June 7, 2012, http://www.mbird.com/2011/09/the-outrageousness-of-gods-indiscriminating-grace-a-brief-interview-with-robert-farrar-capon/?utm_source=twitterfeed&utm_medium=twitter&utm_campaign=Feed%3A+mbird+%28Mockingbird%29.
7. C. S. Lewis, quoted in Philip Yancey, *Where Is God When It Hurts?* (Grand Rapids, MI: Zondervan, 1990), 68.
8. Flannery O'Connor, "On Her Own Work," in *Mystery and Manners* (New York: Farrar, Straus & Giroux, 1957), 112.
9. William James, *Pragmatism: A Series of Lectures by William James* (Rockville, MD: Arc Manor, 2008), 50.
10. Robert Farrar Capon, "The Third Peacock," in *The Romance of the Word: One Man's Love Affair with Theology* (Grand Rapids, MI: Eerdmans, 1995), 222.

PART I:

THE REALITY OF SUFFERING

Each new morn / New widows howl, new orphans cry, new sorrows / Strike heaven upon the face.

—Shakespeare, *Macbeth*

CHAPTER 1

SUFFERING IS INEVITABLE

When you raise children, you hope to shield them from suffering. You do everything in your power to keep painful experiences at bay.

I remember when my boys were little; Nathan was four and Gabe six, and we visited my mom and dad in central Florida. We were inside the house, while the boys played outside with one of the neighborhood kids. When we called them in for dinner, Gabe came running and said, "The boy we were playing with showed me a bad picture." My wife, Kim, ran outside immediately and found that this little seven-year-old boy had a stash of incredibly explicit pornography that he'd probably stolen from his dad.

I wept myself to sleep that night. *They're six and four, and they've already seen this stuff,* I thought. It may seem like a minor incident, but this was the first time that the nastiness and darkness of this world crowded into their innocent, naive world. I couldn't stop thinking about how it could come back to haunt them, that this could be the beginning of a lifelong addiction that could crush them and ruin their marriages. It was devastating to me, and the first time as a parent that I was beside myself. It was merely the tip of the iceberg, but that didn't make it any less painful. I was confronted with the truth that my boys were no more immune to the tragic realities of the world than I was.

Benjamin Franklin memorably captured the inevitability of pain in this life when he wrote, "In this world nothing can be said to be certain, except death and taxes."[1] And while his tone may not necessarily reflect the gravity of the sentiment, he was right. From the death of a loved one, to hurricanes and tsunamis, to the loss of a job, to chronic back pain or inexplicable depression, suffering is everywhere. When the satirical newspaper *The Onion* published the mock headline "Average Time Spent Being Happy Drops to 13 Seconds Per Day,"[2] it confirmed, in a laugh-or-you'll-cry way, what I have learned from fifteen years in ministry. People suffer more deeply and more frequently than they admit, even those who appear to be doing well. In other words, if you're not suffering in some way right now, just wait. Things are not as they should be.

Physical pain and sickness are perhaps the most overt forms of suffering.[3] This ranges from a kindergartner's stubbed toe to a teenager's stress-induced migraines to stomach cancer in old age. It all hurts, and as the multibillion-dollar medical-technology and pharmaceutical industries can attest, we do everything in our power to stave off the decay.

Job himself suffered from excruciating boils, or in more modern language, the sores that form around infected hair follicles. If you know someone who's ever dealt with this affliction, you know that it can be unbearably painful. A friend of mine described his ordeal with a boil on his shoulder as the sensation of a knife being continually jabbed into his back. Imagine that kind of pain across your entire body, and you might have a glimpse into what Job would have suffered. I hope that most of us have not faced the kind of pain and discomfort that Job did—although there are likely female readers who have experienced the intense pain of childbirth and will claim otherwise! But the issue here is not so much the comparative depth of suffering, but simply the fact *that* we suffer. No one is exempt from the dust-to-dust, ashes-to-ashes verdict handed down in the garden of Eden.

Relational suffering is just as universal and severe, though perhaps a bit more elusive. Who hasn't felt misunderstood or taken advantage of? Who hasn't been insulted or cheated or rejected? As life-giving as our relationships with other people can be, they can also be sources of resentment and regret. This form of suffering applies to men and women, children and parents, colleagues at work, and members of your church. The issues involved may be trivial, but the feelings aren't. When a parent misses the game he promised he'd move heaven and earth to attend, it hurts. Getting dumped when you're sixteen years old is extraordinarily painful. So is divorce when you're forty-five. Equally painful are the passive-aggressive comments from a coworker at the office or from the mothers at the playground. And then there's endless stream of "feedback" about how you're filing your TPS reports at work (*Office Space*). This list goes on. Emotional pain is the risk we run when we relate to another person.

Job suffered immensely in this regard. In the midst of all that he had gone through, including loss of home, livelihood, children, and finally, his health, his wife chimed in: "Do you still hold fast your integrity? Curse God and die" (2:9 ESV). Job was already disoriented and alone in his suffering, and the person he loved most told him to just give up, turn his back on God, and die. If there's anyone in Job's life that should have been there to comfort him in his time of blinding agony, it was his wife. The feeling of abandonment must have been terrible. As if that weren't enough, we then read a thirty-odd-chapter conversation between Job and his "friends," in which the friends pick apart every aspect of Job's life in a, frankly, rather creepy kind of spiritual surveillance, looking for some hidden sin they can pin the suffering on. The misguided assumption they are working with, of course, is that nobody suffers these kinds of reversals unless he or she did something to deserve it. We'll return to their ruthless moralizing later. For now, suffice it to say that Job's friends were great counselors—until they opened their mouths! These relational betrayals give a whole new meaning to the phrase "kicking a man when he's down."

This is not to suggest that suffering can ever be neatly organized or clinically categorized. The most tragic events in our lives, such as the sudden death of a loved one, have both physical and emotional components, not to mention spiritual ones, and to the sufferer, the precise makeup is irrelevant. Loss is loss and it stings, pure and simple.

Nicholas Wolterstorff is a Christian who taught philosophical theology for many years at Yale. He and his wife have six children, but he lost an adult son. His son Eric, who was twenty-five at the time, died in a mountain-climbing accident. Wolterstorff chronicled the grief he experienced through his loss in a journal. This is a man who had devoted his life to the understanding, meaning, and reality of life's mysteries, and he suddenly, strikingly, lost a son. In a single moment, all his intellectual categories for making sense of the existence of evil and pain were demolished. He published his journal years later as a book titled *Lament for a Son*. The book opens with his recollection of the moment the dreaded phone call came:

> The call came at 3:30 on that Sunday afternoon, a bright sunny day. We had just sent his younger brother off to the plane to be with him for the summer.
>
> "Mr. Wolterstorff?"
>
> "Yes."
>
> "Is this Eric's father?"
>
> "Yes."
>
> "Mr. Wolterstorff, I must give you some bad news."
>
> "Yes."

> "Eric has been climbing in the mountains and has had an accident."
>
> "Yes."
>
> "Eric has had a serious accident."
>
> "Yes."
>
> "Mr. Wolterstorff, I must tell you, Eric is dead. Mr. Wolterstorff, are you there? You must come at once! Mr. Wolterstorff, Eric is dead."
>
> For three seconds I felt the peace of resignation: arms extended, limp son in hand, peacefully offering him to someone—Someone. Then the pain—cold burning pain.[4]

Wolterstorff's harrowing account explodes the tempting notion that if we only grasped God's will more clearly, if we only knew something we don't know now, the wound would hurt less. But the gospel is not ultimately a defense from pain and suffering; rather, it is the message of God's rescue *through* pain. In fact, it allows us to drop our defenses, to escape not from pain but from the prison of How and Why to the freedom of Who. We are not responsible for finding the right formula to combat or unlock our suffering. The good news of the gospel does not consist of theological assertions or some elaborate religious how-to manual. The good news is Jesus Himself, the Man of Sorrows, the crucified God who meets us in our grief. Indeed, information, even information about Jesus, is relatively useless when it comes to the aching soul. Only the Holy Spirit can comfort a person in the depths of grief. Neil Young claims that "only love can break your heart."[5] But only God can heal it.

Does this mean that the Bible is of no help when it comes to suffering? Of course not! The counterintuitive message of the cross is a message of immense hope and comfort to "those who are perishing." It is not the healthy who need a doctor, after all, but the sick.

FAITH DOES NOT ALWAYS EQUAL PROGRESS

It is not exactly breaking news to say that our culture has an aversion to suffering, regardless of how inescapable it may be. This is because we—*you and me*—have an aversion to suffering. Who wants to suffer? But the conscious avoidance of pain is one thing; the complete intolerance, or outright denial of it, is another. Why do we run so hard from something so inexorable, so much so that we often make the painful situation even worse? Setbacks fly in the face of our dearly held beliefs about progress. They rub against the grain of our collective obsession with personal control, that is, our sin. Celebrated American novelist Jonathan Franzen put it this way:

> We have this notion in this country, not only of endless economic growth but of endless personal growth. I have a certain characterological antipathy to the notion of we're all getting better and better all the time. And it's so clearly belied by our experience. You may get better in certain

> ways for 10 years, but one day you wake up and although things are a little bit different, they're not a lot different.[6]

It's true. Despite the inevitability of suffering, everything in our culture points toward progress, progress, progress. And I'm not just talking about classic rock anthems like The Beatles' "Getting Better," or Fleetwood Mac's "Don't Stop." Unfortunately, our churches often espouse a Christianized version of this gospel of progress, framing the life of belief as primarily about personal improvement. What may start out as a faithful by-product of Christian belief soon becomes its focal point, inadvertently serving as the foothold for Original Sin, aka the innate God complex hiding within us all. Such is the default curved-in-on-itself position of the human heart, or what Augustine termed *incurvatus in se*.

Perhaps you've heard this tendency expressed as a legalistic formula: "The reason for suffering and the lack of abundant life among Christians is due to lack of faith. Or, if you fall ill or come upon hard times financially, maybe it's because there's a hidden skeleton in your closet that needs to be confessed and exposed."

Sadly, such thinking has also seeped into our evangelism: "Accept Jesus as your Lord and Savior, and all your dreams will come true"—despite the fact that the general tenor of the New Testament suggests increased suffering for believers, not decreased. Which isn't to say that Christians never experience victory over areas of compulsive sin and brokenness. They certainly do! But as beautiful and miraculous as these thanksgivings may be, they are not the gospel. In fact, the thinking that ties suffering to faithlessness actually is in the Bible—but it's not affirmed, it's condemned! What *is* affirmed, however, is God working through our afflictions.

This is where Martin Luther, the great leader of the Protestant Reformation, comes in. One of his most important and lasting contributions to the faith involves the distinction between the "theology of glory" and the "theology of the cross." These two divergent views did not originate with Luther. They are as old as the hills; he simply gave them names. It may sound like an esoteric distinction, but it is just as essential today as it was in the sixteenth century.

A THEOLOGY OF GLORY VERSUS A THEOLOGY OF THE CROSS

"Theologies of glory" are approaches to Christianity (and to life) that try in various ways to minimize difficult and painful things, or to move past them rather than looking them square in the face and accepting them. Theologies of glory acknowledge the cross, but view it primarily as a means to an end—an unpleasant but necessary step on the way to personal improvement, the transformation of human potential. As Luther put it, the theologian of glory "does not know God hidden in suffering. Therefore he prefers works to suffering, glory to the cross, strength to weakness, wisdom to folly, and, in general, good to evil."[7] The theology of glory is the natural default setting for human beings addicted to control and measurement. This perspective puts us squarely in the driver's seat, after all.

One way to understand this dynamic is to look at the ways people talk about painful experiences. If someone has just undergone an ugly, protracted divorce, for example, he or she might say something like, "Well, it was never a good marriage anyway," or "But I've really learned a lot from this whole experience."

This kind of rationalization tries to make something bad sound like it is good. It is a strategy to avoid looking pain and grief directly in the face, to avoid acknowledging that we wish life were different but are powerless to change it. In the church, one hallmark of a theology of glory is the unwillingness to acknowledge the reality of ongoing sin and lack of transformation in Christians. A sign that you are operating with a theology of glory is when your faith feels like a fight against these realities instead of a resource for accepting them. The English poet W. H. Auden captured it beautifully when he wrote, "We would rather die in dread / Than climb the cross of the moment / And let our illusions die."[8]

A theology of the cross, in contrast, understands the cross to be the ultimate statement of God's involvement in the world on this side of heaven. A theology of the cross accepts the difficult thing rather than immediately trying to change it or use it. It looks directly into pain, and "calls a thing what it is" instead of calling evil good and good evil. It identifies God as "hidden in [the] suffering."[9] Luther actually took things one key step further. He said that God was not only hidden in suffering, but He was at work in our anxiety and doubt. When you are at the end of your rope—when you no longer have hope within yourself—that is when you run to God for mercy.[10] It's admittedly difficult to accept the claim that God is somehow hidden amid all of the wreckage of our lives. But those who are willing to struggle and despair may in actuality be those among us who best understand the realities of the Christian life.[11]

A theology of the cross defines life in terms of giving rather than taking, self-sacrifice rather than self-protection, dying rather than killing. It reorients us away from our natural inclination toward a theology of glory by showing that we win by losing, we triumph through defeat, and we become rich by giving ourselves away. Of course, our inner theologian of glory can be counted on to try to hijack the theology of the cross and make it a new, more reliable scheme for self-improvement. But the theology of the cross happens *to* us and in spite of us. For the suffering person, this is a word of profound hope.

THE BEST ARGUMENT FOR (AND AGAINST) ATHEISM

In light of the theology of the cross, perhaps it is no coincidence that the apostle Paul wrote, "The foolishness of God is wiser than man's wisdom, and the weakness of God is stronger than man's strength" (1 Cor. 1:25).

Let's look at atheism as a particularly timely example. The best argument for atheism is not the one articulated by Richard Dawkins or Christopher Hitchens. It has nothing to do with logic or rationalism or the laws of physics. No, the best argument for atheism was the one articulated by Ludwig Feuerbach in the nineteenth century, which is the same argument that Karl Marx latched onto and then Sigmund Freud after him (and then Ricky Gervais after him, in his 2009 film *The Invention of Lying*). Simply put, Feuerbach posited that God was a projection of everything good and everything hoped for in the human heart. People take what they value, their dreams, their wishes, and put them in the sky and call them God. God becomes the sum of the things we wish were true. Feuerbach himself wrote:

> God is the Love that satisfies our wishes, our emotional wants; he is himself the realised wish of the heart, the wish exalted to the certainty of its fulfillment, of its reality.[12]

Based on fifteen years of pastoral ministry, I cannot say that Feuerbach's idea is entirely baseless. Certainly you have come across someone who uses God or the Bible in this way. Do you know someone whose picture of God conveniently shares all of his or her personal, political, national, or ideological sympathies? This ranges from the young Christian who tries to cushion a painful breakup by saying that God is "leading me into a season of singleness" (it's rough when God breaks up with you!), to the loving parents who tell their children that "all dogs go to heaven," to churches that preach about God wanting everyone to be rich, to much more serious situations, such as a terrorist looking for justification for taking another's life.

Of course, Mary did not give birth to a projection. She gave birth to a baby boy. And that boy became a man whose existence and impact are verified by numerous historical records outside of the biblical ones. Normally, that's not enough for people. You might hear someone say, "The disciples projected their hopes onto Jesus in their grief" or "Jesus was great; it's Paul that's the problem." Yet even this argument runs into a brick wall when it comes up against the theology of the cross. That is, it loses its strength the moment God is not something we want Him to be. And the crucified God looks like something we would never want. In fact, He is the antithesis of our hopes and dreams. Take for instance, Jesus's saying "Unless a grain of wheat falls into the earth and dies, it remains alone; but if it dies, it bears much fruit" (John 12:24 ESV). Or the psalmist's cry "Let the bones you have crushed rejoice" (Ps. 51:8b). Having to die in order to bear fruit? Bones crushed? That sounds awful! We want pleasure; we want power; we want joy—we do *not* want suffering. And if our relationships and economies are any indication, we prefer a system of fair exchange, of reward and punishment, of deserving, to one of free grace.

No human being would have come up with this idea of God. Nature couldn't teach us the revelation contained in the Bible. I would go so far as to say that the foreign, almost absurd nature of the gospel claim is evidence of its divinity.

A WORD ABOUT *GLORY*

To avoid confusion, a quick word about the term *glory*. It is indeed a biblical word that has its appropriate use. I am aiming to untangle the myriad ways we fuse God's glory with our own glory. So the "glory" in the theology of glory is *human glory focusing on human effort intended to earn God's favor or exalt human achievement.*

The late great Lutheran theologian Gerhard Forde put it like this:

> A theology of glory … operates on the assumption that what we need is optimistic encouragement, some flattery, some positive thinking, some support to build our self-esteem. Theologically speaking it operates on the assumption that we are not seriously addicted to sin, and that our improvement is both necessary and possible. We need a little boost in our desire to do good works.… But the hallmark of a theology of glory is that it will always consider grace as something of a supplement to whatever is left of human will and power.[13]

In the theology of glory, life becomes a ladder. Each little victory or improvement brings us one rung closer to the top—which is always just out of sight. At death, if all goes according to plan, we will enter the heavenly courts with a nicely wrapped gift for God that includes an equitable balance of our good versus bad actions, our moral scorecard, if you will. This image may seem ridiculous, but if we're honest, it characterizes more of our religious life and mentality than we would care to admit. As we tell ourselves this story, we communicate that God exists for our benefit, happiness, self-fulfillment, and personal transformation. Those aren't necessarily bad things, and God isn't necessarily opposed to them, but God in Christ cannot be reduced to a means to our selfish ends. He is the end Himself!

The house of religious cards "that glory built" collapses when we inevitably encounter unforeseen pain and suffering. When the economy tanks and you lose your job of thirty years, or when, God forbid, your child gets into a car accident (or is exposed to something damaging). When you simply can't keep your mouth shut about your in-laws even though you promised you would. When the waters rise and the levee breaks. Suddenly, the mask comes off, and the glory road reaches a dead end. We come to the end of ourselves, in other words, to our ruin, to our knees, to the place where if we are to find any help or comfort, it must come from somewhere outside of us. Much to our surprise, this is the precise place where the good news of the gospel—that God did for you what you couldn't do for yourself—finally makes sense. It finally sounds good!

Yet the message hasn't changed, and neither have the facts. They were there all along. Indeed, *He* was there all along. It might even be that He is communicating the same thing He communicated once for all on Calvary, what Fyodor Dostoyevsky paraphrased so beautifully in the fourth chapter of *The Brothers Karamazov*: "You will burn and you will burn out; you will be healed and come back again."[14]

NOTES

1. Benjamin Franklin (1706–90) used the form we are currently more familiar with, in a letter to Jean-Baptiste Leroy, 1789, which was reprinted in *The Works of Benjamin Franklin*, 1817.
2. "Average Time Spent Being Happy Drops to 13 Seconds per Day," *The Onion*, April 16, 2010, accessed June 4, 2012, http://www.theonion.com/articles/average-time-spent-being-happy-drops-to-13-seconds,17258/.
3. Richard Eyer differentiates between pain and suffering by recalling a pastoral visit to one of his parishioners in the hospital: "Some years ago I visited Jack in the hospital after he broke his leg in a fall at work. He required surgery and a lengthy course of physical therapy. Shortly into therapy it became evident that Jack did not want to overcome his pain and, in fact, needed his pain as an excuse to avoid therapy. Physical therapy would have enabled him to return to a job he hated. Actually, Jack had hoped for a permanent disability due to his accident as a way to free him from his job. Not Jack's pain but the possibility of losing his pain caused Jack's suffering. Pastoral care addressed Jack's suffering, not his pain, and helped him face his anxiety. Jack found spiritual strength to work toward recovery and to return to work.

Attention to suffering is the operating theater of pastoral care" (Richard C. Eyer, *Pastoral Care under the Cross* [St. Louis, MO: Concordia, 1995], 44).

4. Nicholas Wolterstorff, *Lament for a Son* (Grand Rapids, MI: Eerdmans, 1987), 9.
5. Neil Young, "Only Love Can Break Your Heart," *After the Gold Rush* © 1970 Reprise.
6. Jonathan Franzen, interview by Kai Ryssdal, "So Much 'Freedom,' Not a Lot of Happiness," *Marketplace*, September 10, 2010, accessed June 4, 2012, http://www.marketplace.org/topics/life/art-money/so-much-freedom-not-lot-happiness.
7. Martin Luther, "The Heidelberg Disputation, Proof to Thesis 21," *Selected Writings of Martin Luther, 1529–1546*, ed. Theodore G. Tappert (Philadelphia: Fortress, 1967), 79.
8. W. H. Auden, "The Age of Anxiety" in *Collected Poems*, ed. Edward Mendelson (New York: Modern Library, 2007), 530.
9. "Glossary: Theology of Glory," *Mockingbird*, accessed June 4, 2012, http://www.mbird.com/glossary/theology-of-glory/.
10. Luther termed this difficult-to-translate word "Anfechtung," which is most closely related to the concept of *angst*. "God himself must be recognized as the ultimate source of Anfechtung: it is his *opus alienum*, which is intended to destroy man's self-confidence and complacency, and reduce him to a state of utter despair and humiliation, in order that he may finally turn to God, devoid of all the obstacles to

justification which formerly existed. The believer, recognizing the merciful intention which underlies Anfechtung, rejoices in such assaults, seeing in them the means by which God indirectly effects and ensures his salvation. It is for this reason that Luther is able to refer to Anfechtung as a 'delicious despair'. Anfechtung, it must be appreciated, is not some form of spiritual growing pains, which will disappear when a mystical puberty is attained, but a perennial and authentic feature of the Christian life. In order for the Christian to progress in his spiritual life, he must continually be forced back to the foot of the cross, to begin it all over again (*semper a novo incipere*)—and this takes place through the continued experience of Anfechtung" (Alister E. McGrath, *Luther's Theology of the Cross* [Malden, MA: Blackwell, 1985]).

11. "Luther was struggling with a legitimate problem of perspective or standpoint. From God's perspective, the pieces *do* fit together, and one could see God at work even in the trials of our lives. But no human theologian can occupy that perspective, and so, even to make such confident claims is to try to reach beyond faith. By haunting us with the image of that unknown God, Luther reminds Christians of the insecurity with which we must be willing to live if we are to live in trust of a God who remains mystery even in revelation. It may be, he would have claimed, the most insecure among us—the doubters, those who struggle with despair, and those who have most reason to know themselves as

sinners—who are in the best position to understand what living such a Christian life might mean" (William C. Placher, *The Domestication of Transcendence* [Louisville, KY: Westminster John Knox Press, 1996], 51).

12. Ludwig Feuerbach, *The Essence of Christianity*, trans. Marian Evans (London: 1881), Google eBook, 121.
13. Gerhard O. Forde, *On Being a Theologian of the Cross* (Grand Rapids, MI: Eerdmans, 1997), 16.
14. Fyodor Dostoyevsky, *The Brothers Karamazov* (Hertfordshire, UK: Wordsworth Editions, 2007), 23.

CHAPTER 2

SUFFERING IS SERIOUS

Have you ever tried to convince someone who didn't like you that he should? I remember trying in vain to win over a colleague at a former job. Even from our first few encounters, the coldness was apparent whenever we were in the same room. I tried to be charming and funny. I took special care to remember what was going on in this person's life, including his interests and hobbies.

At Christmas I spent extra time buying his gift. I thought about what nice thing I could say that would break the ice. Yet as the months wore on, the situation only seemed to get worse. It soon became a source of real consternation and distraction, the sort of unglamorous, everyday suffering that we tend to brush under the carpet. I was convinced that *if* I only said or did the right thing, *then* this person would like me.

But it didn't work.

In fact, the bad feelings grew until I started to resent him for disliking me! As silly as it sounds, I slowly began to dread going to work. After one particularly transparent overture, a friend pulled me aside and said, "You have to stop this. Everyone sees what you're doing, and it's never going to work. It's not what you do or say that's the issue; it's who you are and what you represent." He was right. I found out later that the person in question had applied for the position I had been given. God used this admittedly low-wattage situation to teach me something important.

"A person with no arms trying to punch themselves until their arms grow back" may be the best description I've ever read of what it feels like for a depressed person to try to cheer herself up.[1] Yet this description applies to any kind of suffering that resists our attempts to address it, both big and small. Grief, anger, and substance abuse are just three particularly potent areas that spring to mind. Far too often we interpret life's defeats as a challenge to pick ourselves up by our bootstraps, dust ourselves off, and get back out there and try a little harder. Disregarding past experience, we make endless resolutions about "next time." We cling to our notions of a universe that runs on the instinctual system of punishment and reward, action and consequence, this for that. We desire a world that we can control, where suffering is a problem to be solved and everyone gets what he or she deserves: this is the gravitational pull of Original Sin. Like Job's friends, we prefer the safety of "if-then" *conditionality*. Suffering, however, often serves as an unwanted reminder that reality does not operate according to our preferences.

Someone once observed that "in the beginning God created man in His image, and ever since, man has been trying to repay the favor." Fortunately for you and me, the God we find in the Bible is not made in our image.

RATCHETING UP THE LAW'S DEMANDS

The God of the Bible is a holy and righteous God. Which is another way of saying that to relate to Him on His own terms, or to receive His blessing, requires perfection. God articulates this perfection in His Law ("Thou shalt" and "Thou shalt not"). The problem is that we are anything but perfect! We are *only* human, as the saying goes. And the divine standard makes painfully clear just how significant our limitations are. The person who takes the Law seriously is immediately humbled, if not demolished completely.

The apostle Paul told us that "whatever the law says, it says to those who are under the law, so that every mouth may be silenced and the whole world held accountable to God" (Rom. 3:19). If we are to relate to God, or if God is to relate to us, it must be through some form of mediating forgiveness. That relationship must come from something other than what we bring to the table.

At the risk of oversimplification, in the Old Testament, the Israelites could receive God's forgiveness and approval only through complicated rituals of sacrifice and repentance. Yet even these religious guidelines proved too difficult. You might say that when it came to God's Law, we define the Israelites by their failure. So it might seem strange that centuries later, Jesus came along and ratcheted up the demand.

"You have heard that it was said.... But I tell you" (Matt. 5:21–22). That's right. Jesus is neither the Grumpy Grandfather in the Sky who sends down lightning bolts to smite those who fail to keep His Law nor the Cool Cosmic Uncle who pats us on the back and just gives us a pass on all that righteousness stuff. Instead, in the Sermon on the Mount, Jesus said that if you have hate in your heart, it is the same thing as committing murder. He equated lustful glances with adulterous acts. Was He exaggerating things for the sake of His dense listeners? Or was He trying to say that in God's eyes, the internal and the external are of equal importance? Much as we would like to wriggle free (and much as we try to!), the Law is not superficial. It applies as much to motivation as action. It may sound harsh, but the same is true of our other relationships. All the flowers and phone calls in the world don't amount to "a hill of beans" if there's no love behind them; you can always tell when someone is calling because he wants something from you or if he genuinely cares about how you are doing.

Who, then, can be saved? In Matthew 19:26, Jesus said that "with man this is impossible, but with God all things are possible."

Perhaps an illustration will help. Imagine a man standing at the gates of heaven, waiting for admittance. Peter greets him by saying, "You have to have earned a thousand points to get in. What have you done to earn your points?"

Somewhat taken aback, the man answers, "I've never heard that before, but let me see … I was raised in a Christian home and have always been a part of the church. I have Sunday school attendance pins that go down the floor. I went to a Christian college and graduate school and have led hundreds of people to

Christ. Before I died, I was an elder in my church and supportive of the people of God. I have three children, two boys and a girl. My oldest boy is a pastor, and the younger has a ministry to the poor. My daughter and her husband are missionaries. I have always tithed, giving as much as 30 percent of my income to God's work at the end. In my job as a bank executive, I worked with the poor in our city who were trying to get low-income mortgages."

"How am I doing so far?" he asked Peter.

"That's one point," Peter said. "What else have you done?"

"Good Lord … have mercy!" the man said in frustration.

"That's it!" Peter said. "Welcome home."

This story may be a bit corny, but the underlying truth is not. The Law exists to extinguish any sense that we can "git 'er done," and the only sane response to its comprehensive demand is a cry for mercy. The Law brings us to our knees, revealing to believers and unbelievers alike who we really are—namely, sinners in need of a savior. It is the schoolmaster that teaches us just how much we need to receive from Jesus: *everything*.

THE IMMORALITY OF (MERE) MORALITY

When we blunt the Law in any way, when we file its "teeth" down, or when we insert qualifications to make its commands more palatable, it quickly becomes a tool of the self-justifying sinner.

If, for instance, Christ's injunctions in the Sermon on the Mount are explained away or somehow softened—surely He cannot mean we should be perfect!—if the door is held open even a little, we will hold on for dear life to whatever merits we can achieve for ourselves. Not only that, we make sure everyone around us does the same. Our feeble attempts at holiness become the basis of our faith, rather than the One who justifies the ungodly. The sufferer will keep himself or herself on life support rather than trust in the One who raises the dead. Sadly, such is often the modus operandi we find on Sunday morning. The tragic irony of legalism is not that it has too large a view of the Law, but too small of one! A softened view of the Law creates a culture of judgmental hypocrisy. A purer view creates a culture of humble transparency, even and especially when it comes to our various hypocrisies.

Think about it: Do you walk out of church feeling burdened or comforted? Does your pastor direct you inward or outward? Does the worship service revolve around the Christian or Christ Himself?

I recently received a letter that captures this dynamic with deep insight:

> Over the last couple of years, [my wife and I] have been struggling with the preaching in our church. After listening, I feel condemned and powerless. Spiritually, I've become very depressed, to the point where I had no desire even to attend church.... [Hearing the gospel of grace has been] like a fresh ocean breeze blowing [on] my face.

> The focus on the finished work of Christ points us away from ourselves, and gradually I have found myself crawling out of my spiritual depression and wanting to do the things God has called me to do. This isn't a result of more law in my life, but more gospel.

This dear Christian has come to understand the irony hinted at above. Legalism doesn't make people "better"; it makes them worse. Moralism doesn't produce morality; it produces immorality. We make a terrible mistake when we believe that the answer to poor performance, be it moral, spiritual, or relational, is more Law. People get worse, not better, when you lay down the Law.

Think about it in your own life. Have you ever given someone an ultimatum? Has anyone ever given you one? The fruit of scrutiny and judgment in relationships, even the most well-intentioned kind, is resentment and distance, not deeper closeness. The Law, in other words, can be a vehicle for suffering. Perhaps this is why Paul wrote about how "the law was added so that the trespass might increase" (Rom. 5:20a).

This is not to say that the Law is somehow bad or negative. Quite the contrary, the Law is good and holy! If we were able to obey it, we would indeed live in total harmony with God, ourselves, and other people. Just because no one has cured cancer does not mean that it wouldn't be a wonderful thing were it to happen. Indeed, the Spirit uses both the Law and the gospel in our lives; He just uses them differently. The Law *reveals* sin but is powerless to *remove* it. The Law *points* to righteousness but can't *inspire* it. It shows us what godliness is, but it cannot make us godly. The Law, in this sense, is incapable of producing what it demands—it is impotent. It has no strength or power to improve a person, nor was it meant to. The eighteenth-century poet and hymnodist John Berridge summed it up beautifully:

To run and work the Law commands,
Yet gives me neither feet nor hands;
A sweeter thing the Gospel brings—
It bids me fly and gives me wings![2]

So, the Law shows us how to love God and others and, in doing so, reveals how short we fall each and every day—in fact, if we're honest, most of the time we don't even want to try. Yet when we fail, the gospel surprises us with the news that God's approval does not depend on our obedience but on Christ's. Which is more than exciting, it is inspiring!

Take the award-winning 2011 documentary *Buck*, about legendary horse trainer Buck Brannaman. At the beginning of the film, we find out that Buck and his older brother spent their childhoods as trick-roping child prodigies, touring the country doing their lasso routine, appearing on television, and competing. But then we find out the chilling reason for their success, as Buck describes in some detail the terrifying home life they experienced in the wake of their mother's death. If the boys made a false move in their act, their alcoholic father would beat them within an inch of their lives. He was the Law incarnate (You Must Be Perfect … *or Else*).

At long last, a football coach notices the bruises and welts on Buck's body, and immediately contacts the police. They take the boys to live with a foster family, and in the film, Buck shares about his first encounter with his foster father:

> When I first got dropped off at my [foster parents'] ranch, I was so terrified of men. My foster dad-to-be, he pulled up in his truck, and he was tall … looked like he was made out of rawhide and barbed wire—but he walked right up to me and said "You must be Buck." I shook his hand, but I couldn't even speak. You can be so scared that you can't say anything.… I just sat there. And my little knees were just about knocking together.… He spun around, walked back to the truck and opened the door. And my heart just stopped.… He threw me a pair of buckskin gloves. He said, "Here. You're gonna need them." And they were just beautiful and they fit me perfect.… We took off and we built fence all afternoon. But I wouldn't wear those gloves. They were a token act of kindness.… I didn't want to get them tore up. I put them in my pocket, and I worked the barbed wire all day with my bare hands.[3]

In Buck's life, grace accomplishes what the Law never could—a heart that desires to obey. Indeed, it is "God's kindness [that] leads you toward repentance" (Rom. 2:4).

LAW BEYOND THE TEN COMMANDMENTS

When talking about "the law," we need to make an important distinction. It is the distinction between big *L* Law and little *l* law. Big *L* Law comes from God and is outlined in the Ten Commandments, reiterated in the Sermon on the Mount, and summarized by Jesus as the command to "'love the Lord your God with all your heart and with all your soul and with all your strength and with all your mind'; and, 'Love your neighbor as yourself'" (Luke 10:27). But there's another law (little *l*) that plays out in all kinds of ways in daily life. Paul Zahl put it this way:

> Law with a small "l" refers to an interior principle of demand or ought that seems universal in human nature. In this sense, law is any voice that makes us feel we must do something or be something to merit the approval of another. For example, what we shall call "the law of capability" is the demand a person may feel that he/she be 100% capable in everything he/she does—or else! In the Bible, the Law comes from God. In daily living, law is an internalized principle of self-accusation. We might

> say that the innumerable laws we carry inside us are bastard children of the Law.[4]

No one understood the dynamic of how the accusation of the law functions in the human psyche better than Martin Luther. He characterized the law as "a voice that man can never stop in this life,"[5] one that can be heard anywhere and everywhere, not just on Sunday morning. It takes any number of forms, but its function remains the same: *it accuses*. Indeed, the "oughts" of life are as numerous as they are oppressive: infomercials promising a better life if you work at getting a better body. A neighbor's new car, a beautiful person, the success of your coworker—all these things have the potential to communicate that "you are not enough."

The other day I drove down the road near my house and passed a sign in front of a store that read, "Life is the art of drawing without an eraser." Meant to inspire drivers-by to work hard, live well, and avoid mistakes, it served as a booming voice of law to everyone who read it: "Don't mess up. There are no second chances. You better get it right the first time." Again, Paul Zahl chimed in insightfully:

> In practice, the requirement of perfect submission to the commandments of God is exactly the same as the requirement of perfect submission to the innumerable drives for perfection that drive everyday people's crippled and crippling lives. The commandment of God that we honor our

> father and mother is no different *in impact*, for example, than the commandment of fashion that a woman be beautiful or the commandment of culture that a man be boldly decisive and at the same time utterly tender.[6]

The world is full to the brim with law. Not just laws of Scripture, laws of science, and tax codes, but lesser, subjective laws. And they cause us enormous grief. Indeed, identity is an area of life frequently mired in legalities: "I must be a __________ kind of person, and not a __________ kind of person if I'm ever going to be somebody."

An environment of law, as we all know, is an environment of fear. We are afraid of the judgment that the law wields. Or as the poet Czeslaw Milosz described in his poem "A Many-Tiered Man": "[Man] is frightened of a verdict, / now, for instance, / or after his death."

We instinctually know that if we don't measure up, the judge will punish us. When we feel this weight of judgment against us, we all tend to slip into the slavery of self-salvation: trying to appease the judge (friends, parents, spouse, and ourselves) with hard work, good behavior, getting better, achievement, losing weight, and so on. We conclude: "If I can just stay out of trouble and get good grades, maybe my mom and dad will finally approve of me. If I can overcome this addiction, then I'll be able to accept myself. If I can get thin, maybe my husband will finally think

I'm beautiful. If I can make a name for myself and be successful, maybe I'll get the respect I long for."

The law stifles and causes us to second-guess ourselves. Have you ever found yourself writing and rewriting the same email over and over again? Or procrastinating when making an important phone call? The recipient almost inevitably has become a stand-in for the law. We put people in this role with alarming facility.

The idea of "law" simply makes sense, and universally so. The apostle Paul even claimed that it is written on the heart (Rom. 2:15). In fact, those who don't believe in God tend to struggle with self-recrimination and self-hatred just as much as those who do; no one is free of guilt—the law is not subject to our belief in it. Some of us even compound our failures and suffering by heaping judgment upon judgment, intoxicated by the voice of "not-enoughness," not content until we have usurped the role of the One who is actually qualified to pass a sentence.

In a 2005 interview with journalist Michka Assayas, U2 lead singer Bono spoke eloquently about law and grace in terms of karma:

> At the center of all religions is the idea of Karma. You know, what you put out comes back to you: an eye for an eye, a tooth for a tooth, or in physics—in physical laws—every action is met by an equal or an opposite one. It's clear to me that Karma is at the very heart of the Universe.

> I'm absolutely sure of it. And yet, along comes this idea called Grace to upend all that "As you reap, so will you sow" stuff. Grace defies reason and logic. Love interrupts, if you like, the consequences of your actions, which in my case is very good news indeed, because I've done a lot of stupid stuff.... I'd be in big trouble if Karma was going to finally be my judge.... It doesn't excuse my mistakes, but I'm holding out for Grace. I'm holding out that Jesus took my sins onto the Cross, because I know who I am, and I hope I don't have to depend on my own religiosity.[7]

GRACE: TOPPLING THE ECONOMY OF REWARD AND PUNISHMENT

Against the tumult of conditionality—punishment and reward, score keeping, karma, you-get-what-you-deserve, big *L* Law, little *l* law, whatever name you choose—comes the second of God's two words, His *grace*. Grace is the gift with no strings attached. It is one-way love. It is what makes the good news so good, the once-for-all proclamation that there is "now no condemnation for those who are in Christ Jesus" (Rom. 8:1).

The gospel of grace announces that Jesus came to acquit the guilty—He came to judge and be judged in our place. Christ came to satisfy the deep judgment against us once and for all so that we could be free from the judgment of God, others, and ourselves. He came to give rest to our efforts at trying to deal with judgment on our own. The gospel declares that Jesus atoned for our guilt and that the Law has been fulfilled. So we don't need to live under the burden of trying to appease the judgment we feel; in Christ the ultimate demand has been met, the deepest judgment satisfied. The internal voice that says, "Do this and live," gets shouted down by the external voice that says, "It is finished!"

Yet there is nothing harder for us to wrap our minds around than the unconditional, contingent-free grace of God. In fact, it "defies our reason and logic," upending our sense of fairness and offending our deepest intuitions, especially when it comes to those who have done us harm. Like Job's friends, we insist that reality operate according to the predictable economy of reward and punishment. Like the elder brother in the parable of the prodigal son, we have worked too hard to give up now. The storm may rage all around us, our foundations may shake, but we would rather perish than give up our "rights."

Yet still the grace of God prevails! His gracious disposition toward us thankfully does not depend even on our ability to comprehend it. When we finally come to the end of ourselves, there He will be. Just as He will be the next time we come to the end of ourselves, and the time after that, and the time after that. Indeed, we never come to a point in our lives where we no longer need God's grace, and fortunately, it knows no end. A word of caution from Robert Capon before we move on:

> The Gospel of grace must not be turned into a bait-and-switch offer. It is not one of those airline supersavers in which you read of a $59.00 fare to Orlando only to find, when you try to buy a ticket, that the six seats per flight at that price are all taken and that the trip will now cost you $199.95. Jesus must not be read as having baited us with grace only to clobber us in the end with law. For as the death and resurrection of Jesus were accomplished once and for all, so the grace that reigns by those mysteries reigns eternally—even in the thick of judgment.[8]

WHAT DOES THIS HAVE TO DO WITH SUFFERING?

Everything! The gospel frees us to speak honestly about the reality of pain, confident that nothing rides on our ability to cope with or fend off suffering. Before we can even begin to grapple with the frustrations and tragedies of life in this world, we must do away with our faithless morality of payback and reward. We must reacquaint ourselves with the biblical weight of the problem that we less-than-perfect human beings are contending with in the face of a holy and righteous God. We must return to the beginning (and end) of the whole affair: the cross. And by the power of the Holy Spirit, we must pray that our eyes would be opened, that we would see the crucifixion for what it is, not looking away, or through, or past it. Because that's when we begin to realize how amazing His grace really is. Thank the Lord that He doesn't count our sins against us! Praise God for settling the score and closing the accounts, once for all! Hallelujah! Grace is the opposite of what we deserve, and it is exactly what we get.

For those who are suffering, my hope is that clearing away the clutter of this nefarious idea of cosmic payback is a relief.

If you have suffered the loss of a family member to chronic disease, if you suffer debilitating seasons of depression, if you lost your job and livelihood, or if you went through a divorce that came out of the blue, know that God is not punishing you. He is not waiting for you to do something. You don't have to pull yourself up by your bootstraps and find a way to conquer the odds, be stronger, or transform yourself into some better version of yourself. The pain you feel (whatever the degree) may be a reminder that things are not as they should be, in which case it is appropriate to mourn the gravity of that brokenness.

While God does indeed use the suffering in our lives, He is interested in much more than improvements in your personality or circumstantial happiness; He is interested in *saving* you. He is more than your Helper; He is your Redeemer. We do not have the primary role in this drama after all; we are the actors, not the directors. Sometimes it requires getting on our knees for us to see the truth.

My prayer for you is that as you continue reading, you will begin to comprehend the height, depth, and length of the love of Jesus right in the very middle of your present suffering.

NOTES

1. Allie, "Adventures in Depression," *Hyberbole and a Half,* accessed June 4, 2012, http://hyperboleandahalf.blogspot.com/2011/10/adventures-in-depression.html.
2. Quoted in F. F. Bruce, *Romans,* Tyndale New Testament Commentary, rev. ed. (Grand Rapids, MI: Eerdmans, 1985), 154. Some attribute the poem to John Bunyan. Ralph Erskine (1685–1752) has a similar poem in his gospel sonnets: "A rigid matter was the law, demanding brick, denying straw. But when with gospel tongue it sings, it bids me fly and gives me wings" (*The Sermons and Practical Works of Ralph Erskine,* vol. 10 [Glasgow: W. Smith and J. Bryce, 1778], 283).
3. Buck Brannaman, *Buck,* directed by Cindy Meehl (New York: ICF Films, 2011). Quote from "The Gospel According to *Buck*: Grace with Gloves and Jesus with Horses," *Mockingbird,* January 9, 2012, accessed June 4, 2012, http://www.mbird.com/2012/01/the-gospel-according-to-buck-grace-with-gloves-and-jesus-with-horses/.
4. Paul Zahl, *Who Will Deliver Us?* (Eugene, OR: Wipf & Stock, 2008), 6.
5. Martin Luther, quoted in Gerhard O. Forde, *Where God Meets Man: A Down-to-Earth Approach to the Gospel* (Minneapolis: Augsburg, 1977), 15.
6. Paul Zahl, *Grace in Practice: A Theology of Everyday Life* (Grand Rapids, MI: Eerdmans, 2007), 29.

7. Bono, quoted in Michka Assayas, *Bono: Conversations with Michka Assayas (*New York: Penguin, 2006), Google eBook.
8. Robert Farrar Capon, *Kingdom, Grace, and Judgment: Paradox, Outrage and Vindication in the Parables of Jesus* (Grand Rapids, MI: Eerdmans, 2002), 355.

CHAPTER 3

SUFFERING HONESTLY

There is a classic, virtually wordless *Calvin and Hobbes* comic strip that sums up what life often feels like. It's a series of panels, each depicting a scene from a single day. First, Calvin sits on a wad of bubble gum. Next, his teacher catches him glancing at his classmate's paper. Then a bully knocks him down in the hallway. The water fountain sprays in his face. The bug he'd brought in for show-and-tell escapes. He gets picked last at recess. There's a hair in his lunch, and when he heads to the swing set, all the seats are occupied. Finally, he misses the bus and has to walk home in the rain. In his bedroom that evening, Calvin looks at his trusted tiger and says, "You know, Hobbes, some days even my lucky rocketship underpants don't help."

We've all had the adult version of one of those days. It doesn't just rain—it comes down in buckets. Traffic on your commute is bumper to bumper, and parking spaces are curiously sparse. Your spouse counts on you to get home early so you can look after the kids while she attends an important meeting. You've been running late a lot recently, so she reminds you more than once that this meeting simply cannot be missed. On your way out of the office, the coworker you've been avoiding all day/week/year corners you, and suddenly you find yourself in one of "those" conversations. You know the kind of conversation I mean, and you know they are never quick or easy.

Thirty minutes later you sit in a cold sweat in the middle of stop-and-go traffic in the midst of a downpour. In your rush to make it home, you slip into the carpool lane to make up for lost time, you know, just this once. But as you pull into the lane—slam! One of your rain-blurred fellow commuters comes out of nowhere and rear-ends you. Now you're really late! Not that it matters to the officer writing up the accident, who makes a point of giving you a citation for driving in the carpool lane. As if that weren't enough, you forgot to charge your cell phone at the office and you watch helplessly as it powers down.

Meanwhile your spouse sits at home, simultaneously scanning the driveway and mentally signing your death warrant. You finally make it home an hour late, explain the preposterous-sounding sequence of events over a tense and lukewarm dinner. An hour later the kids are off to bed, and you can finally relax, at least after you finally deal with the passive-aggressive voice mail you got from your brother-in-law earlier that day. But guess what? There's been an outbreak of flu at school, and your kids unfortunately weren't spared. The vomiting starts at nine and does not stop until two.

I exaggerate, but only slightly.

We each have days that couldn't end quickly enough, days where we throw up our hands and say that we'll try again tomorrow. These are days full of the sort of curveballs that make you wish you'd stayed in bed, and frayed nerves and ill-advised attempts to reverse the tide often compound your exasperation. Everything snowballs into one big heap of exhaustion. Make no mistake—the individual factors may be trifling, but the suffering is all too real. Sure, there's not anything particularly dramatic or glamorous about such everyday misfortune, but that does not invalidate it. When we resist classifying it as suffering, we embrace the misconception that God is interested only in the more tragic situations of our lives. Yet so often the little things *are* the big things.

I do not mean to trivialize suffering or suggest that broken fingernails are the same as broken hearts. In fact, the intent here is the opposite: to broaden our understanding of suffering in the hopes of being a bit more honest with God and ourselves. I wrote previously that suffering is inevitable and that it is universal. I'd like to go one step further and say that everyone is suffering in some way, today, right now. Perhaps your situation is dire: a death in the family, a painful heartbreak, the loss of a job, a wayward teenager. Maybe your situation is relatively innocuous: a harshly worded email, a few extra pounds on the scale that won't go away, or an unexpected car-maintenance bill. All of this is suffering, and all of it is proof that the world is not as it should be!

The poet and memoirist Mary Karr said it this way:

> The most privileged, comfortable person … from the best family, has already suffered the

> torments of the damned. I don't think any of us get off this planet without suffering enormously. And one of the chief ways we suffer is by loving people who are incredibly limited by the fact that they're human beings, and they're going to disappoint us and break our hearts.... We are all heartbroken.[1]

Perhaps this is self-evident. Yet religious people in particular have a tough time being honest about their suffering. Occasionally we can even foster an environment of denial. In the church, one hallmark of a theology of glory is the unwillingness to acknowledge the reality of ongoing sin and suffering and lack of "victory" in Christians. So before we continue to talk about the ways we deal with suffering, let's explore the ways we *don't* deal with it.

A FEW BARRIERS TO HONESTY

The first barrier to honesty is this: we project a hierarchy of suffering onto God Himself. Someone recently forwarded me a particularly vivid example of this method of denial: "If anyone is having a bad day, remember that in 1976 Ronald Wayne sold his 10% stake in Apple for $800. Now it's worth $58,065,210,000."

Translated into spiritual terms you might say, "I'm having a bad day, but at least I don't have pancreatic cancer. God has too much on His plate for me to bother Him with my petty concerns. He clearly cares more about starving children than He does about my seasonal depression." There may be something noble about keeping things in proper perspective, but soon we are dictating to God what He should or shouldn't care about. And it is a slippery slope! Eventually we'll edit our prayers along these lines, as though we were giving a political speech, rather than simply speaking with our heavenly Father. If the only things that qualify as suffering in your life are natural disasters or global warfare, you will soon find yourself plastering a smile on your face and nodding overenthusiastically whenever someone asks you how you are doing.

Shiny, happy Christians are insufferable, pun intended.

The second barrier is related and, like the first, by no means restricted to Christians. We establish other boundaries for suffering, such as time limits and phraseology. In his book *Shattered Dreams*, Larry Crabb related hearing a pastor say, "We must pray for our dear sister. She lost her husband two months ago and is still battling grief. She should be over it by now."[2]

Grief, of course, is not something that operates according to a specific time frame, and it seems cold to suggest otherwise. Yet when we do not grasp that God is present in pain, we eventually insist on victory or, worse, blame the sufferer for not "getting over it" fast enough. This is more than a failure to extend compassion; it's an exercise in cruelty.

Or maybe the "should" (the little *l* law) takes the form of an insistence on a proper way to suffer. "Real men don't cry," or "In my family we keep a stiff upper lip." For instance, small-group

Bible studies can be wonderful times of mutual encouragement and spiritual edification.

They can also be highly sanitized group-enabling sessions, governed by a suffocating set of unwritten rules about what is permissible and what is not. Maybe you are allowed to voice a prayer concern only if it's couched in hopeful terms. "My wife and I have been going through a tough season recently, but I know God uses iron to sharpen iron." Instead of, say, "My wife and I can't stop fighting. We are at each other's throats night and day, and I don't know how much more I can take. We both know it's not good, but we can't seem to help ourselves. I don't know what to do." When an admission of suffering or weakness is interpreted as a lack of faith, honesty soon falls by the wayside, leaving the sufferer lonelier than before. There must be a Good Friday before there can be an Easter, and if our suffering is hedged in language intended to shield God from culpability, we never get beyond the life-support stage.

Behind each one of these barriers to honesty is a deep-seated misconception about Christianity. Contrary to popular belief, Christianity is not about good people getting better. If anything, it is about bad people coping with their failure to be good. That is to say, Christianity concerns the gospel, which is nothing more or less than the good news that "Christ Jesus came into the world to save sinners" (1 Tim. 1:15). "[Christ] was delivered over to death for our sins and was raised to life for our justification" (Rom. 4:25). The gospel is a proclamation that always addresses sinners and sufferers directly (i.e., you and me).

The prevailing view in much of contemporary Christianity is more subjective. It tends to be far more focused on the happiness and moral performance of the Christian than the object of faith, Christ Himself.

Think about it: How often have you heard the gospel equated with a positive change in a believer's life? "I used to ___________, but then I met Jesus and now I'm ___________." It may be unintentional, but we make a serious mistake when we reduce the good news to its results, such as patience, sobriety, and compassion, in the lives of those who have heard it. These are beautiful developments, and they should be celebrated. But they should not be confused with the gospel itself. The gospel is not a means to an end, it is an end in itself.

What happens in this scheme is the following: well-meaning Christians adopt a narrative of improvement that becomes a law (or an identity, which is often the same thing) through which we filter our experiences. The narrative can be as simple as "I was worse, but now I am better," or as arbitrary as "I used to have a difficult relationship with my mother, but now it's much easier." Soon we wed our faith to these narratives, and when an experience or feeling doesn't fit—for example, when we have a sudden outburst of anger at someone we thought we had forgiven—we deny or rationalize the behavior.

If the narrative we've adopted says that in order for our relationship with God to be legitimate, our life *has* to get better and our suffering get smaller, we set up an inescapable conflict, or what social scientists call "cognitive dissonance." When our view of ourselves is at risk, honesty is always the first casualty. That is, when the gospel is twisted into a moral improvement scheme, (self-)deception is the foregone conclusion.

There's a classic *New Yorker* cartoon of a man sitting down with a woman, having dinner, saying to her, "Look, I can't promise I'll change, but I can promise I'll pretend to change."[3] I hope that line doesn't characterize your church, but it does characterize more churches than you think. Instead of a hospital for sufferers, church becomes a glorified costume party, where lonely men and women tirelessly police each other's facade of holiness. The higher up in the pecking order, the less room for weakness. Perhaps it should come as no surprise when we read headlines of pastors of legalistic churches acting out in self-destructive ways (Rom. 5:20).

THE END OF ACCOUNTABILITY

One of the chief vehicles for denial of suffering in my own life has been my involvement in "accountability groups." For those who have been spared them, an "accountability group" is a single-sex small-group Bible study on steroids. A group of friends arrange for a time each week to get together, ostensibly to encourage one another by upholding standards of personal righteousness in a confidential context.

Instead, the members spend most of the time picking each other apart, uncovering layer after layer after layer of sin in a coercive and sometimes even competitive fashion. You confess your sin to your friends and they to you, and at first it's a relief. Light shines into dark corners, and you pray honestly for the first time in ages. You may even find yourself a bit less drawn to whatever behavior brought you to the group in the first place. As the weeks wear on and you find that your victory was more short-lived than you had initially hoped, perhaps you start to embellish or hold back in order to concoct some narrative of improvement. Or perhaps you remain entirely truthful, but your friends begin to doubt your sincerity. Soon nothing is enough; no matter what you unveil, they look for you to uncover something deeper, darker, and more embarrassing than what you've already shared. You start to embellish in the other direction, anything that will make the others feel better about themselves. Eventually everyone is investigating one another, and no one is telling the truth.

Well, I can't stand those groups!

Setting aside the obvious objection that Christ settled all our accounts, once for all, such groups inevitably start with the narcissistic presupposition mentioned earlier—simply that Christianity is all about cleaning up and doing your part. These groups focus primarily (in my experience, almost exclusively) on our sin, and not on our Savior. Because of this, they breed self-righteousness, guilt, and the almost irresistible temptation to pretend, or to be less than honest. Little or no attention is given to the gospel. There's no reminder of what Christ has done for our sin—cleansing us from its guilt and power—and of the resources that are already ours by virtue of our union with Him. These groups thrive, either intentionally or not, on a "do more, try harder" moralism that robs us of the joy and freedom Jesus paid dearly to secure for us.

When the goal becomes conquering our sin instead of soaking in the conquest of our Savior, we actually begin to shrink spiritually. Sinclair Ferguson rightly pointed this out:

> Those who have almost forgotten about their own spirituality because their focus is so exclusively on their union with Jesus Christ and what He has accomplished are those who are growing and exhibiting fruitfulness. Historically speaking, whenever the piety of a particular group is focused on OUR spirituality that piety will eventually exhaust itself on its own resources. Only where our piety forgets about ourself and focuses on Jesus Christ will our piety [be] nourished by the ongoing resources the Spirit brings to us from the source of all true piety, our Lord Jesus Christ.[4]

The tragic irony in all of this is that when we focus so strongly on our need to get better, *we actually get worse*. We become even more neurotic and self-absorbed. Preoccupation with our guilt (instead of God's grace) makes us increasingly self-centered and morbidly introspective. And what is Original Sin if not a preoccupation with ourselves? What needs to be rooted out and attacked is not immoral behavior; it's immoral belief—faith in my own moral and spiritual "progress," rather than in the One who died to atone for my lack of progress.

I've said it once and I'll say it again and again, because I need to be reminded myself: Christianity is not first and foremost about our behavior, our obedience, our response, and our daily victory over sin. It is first and foremost about Jesus! It is about His person; His substitutionary work; His incarnation, life, death, resurrection, ascension, and promised return. We are justified—and sanctified—by grace alone through faith alone in the finished work of Christ alone. Even now, the banner under which Christians live reads, "It is finished." Everything we need, and everything we look for in things smaller than Jesus, is already ours in Christ.

Therefore the accountability we really need is the kind that corrects our natural tendency to dwell on me—my obedience (or lack thereof), my performance (good or bad), my holiness—instead of on Christ and His obedience, His performance, and His holiness for me. It sometimes seems that we can't help ourselves from turning the good news of God's grace into a narcissistic program of self-improvement. We try to turn grace into law, in other words. We need to be held accountable for that! The gravitational pull of conditionality is so strong, our hardwiring for law so ingrained, that we need real friends to remind us of the good news every day. In fact, our lives depend on it! So instead of trying to fix one another, perhaps we might try "stirring one another up to love and good deeds" by daily reminding one another, in humble love, of the riches we already possess in Christ. If we have to label them, we can call them "comfort groups" or maybe "transparency groups."

There are myriad secular versions of "accountability groups." After all, it's not the Christian heart that is attracted to control and law—it is the *human* heart. "Accountability" is even something of a buzzword in contemporary management science. Just peruse the self-help aisle next time you're in a bookstore, and you will find a depressing number of examples—books that promise to change you via elaborate accountability structures. Timothy Ferriss's *4-Hour Body*, for example, suggests that to get your dream body, you must commit to weighing yourself every morning, keeping a strict journal of what you eat, and even photographing all your meals before you dig in! If that's not accountability, I don't know what is. And if you were to follow his instructions, no doubt you *would* lose weight (and people do). The problem comes, as with the Law of God, when you find that you can't. And indeed, the real question when it comes to dieting is never, "Will this program help me lose weight?" The real question is always, "Will the program help me keep the weight off once I lose it?"

The bottom line is that rules and regulations (and the resulting guilt) are not enough to change our hearts. Only grace has that power.

Think about your experience with social media. Some might say that Facebook has turned our lives into one never-ending accountability group, with our profiles functioning as the "self" we present to the world for measurement and scrutiny. Don't get me wrong—I like Facebook as much as the next guy. But I can't help but agree with the journalist who wrote that the "price of this smooth sociability is a constant compulsion to assert one's own happiness, one's own fulfillment.... Being happy all the time, pretending to be happy, actually attempting to be happy—it's exhausting."[5] An understatement, to say the least! But it's more than exhausting. Like legalistic accountability groups with its me-focus on behavior (and appearance), Facebook can breed dishonesty and loneliness. In the book *Alone Together: Why We Expect More from Technology and Less from Each Other*, Sherry Turkle speaks about one of her interview subjects, a middle-school student named Brad:

> Brad says, only half jokingly, that he worries about getting "confused" between what he "composes" for his online life and who he "really" is. Not yet confirmed in his identity, it makes him anxious to post things about himself that he doesn't really know are true. It burdens him that the things he says online affect how people treat him in the real. People already relate to him based on things he has said on Facebook. Brad struggles to be more "himself" there, but this is hard. He says that even when he tries to be "honest" on Facebook, he cannot resist the temptation to use the site "to make the right impression."[6]

As if that's not enough, a study published in *Cyberpsychology, Behavior, and Social Networking* in 2012 found that the more time people spent on Facebook, the happier they perceived their friends to be and the sadder they felt as a consequence.[7] Perhaps it is no coincidence that a wise man once said that the Law kills (2 Cor. 3:6).

To be clear, I absolutely believe in our collective need to repent and confess our sins to one another (James 5:16). I am only cautioning against doing so outside the context of the countervailing, scandalous nature of God's unconditional love. It is, after all, "God's kindness [that] leads you toward repentance" (Rom. 2:4), repentance being nearly synonymous with honesty. The confidence that "there is now no condemnation for those who are in Christ Jesus" (Rom. 8:1) is the engine that fuels honesty with one another, about both our ongoing sin and our ongoing suffering. Fortunately, this is the good news that lies at the heart of the gospel. But I digress.

NOT AS IT SHOULD BE

As we have established, ongoing suffering is not imaginary. Whether you are a Christian or not, none of us has ever known a day in which suffering is altogether absent. Admitting this reality is in no way an indicator of a lack of faith. Quite the opposite! By way of a quick refresher: in the beginning, God designed the world in such a way that there would be peace and harmony in His world. Life under God's gracious rule is beautiful, and its enjoyment is called *shalom*. One scholar wrote:

> In the Bible, shalom means *universal flourishing, wholeness, and delight*—a rich state of affairs in which natural needs are satisfied and natural gifts fruitfully employed, a state of affairs that inspires joyful wonder as its Creator and Savior opens doors and welcomes the creatures in whom he delights. Shalom, in other words, is the way things ought to be.[8]

What you and I now experience is a state of "antishalom." In most cases, this wrecking of shalom is personal. When someone sins against us or harms us, whatever was done to us violates God's shalom. Whether it's relational strain, sexual abuse, or murder—it's all a violation. But there is a larger aspect to this. As Romans 8 indicates, all creation is fallen, groaning in anticipation of its redemption.[9]

> The creation waits with eager longing for the revealing of the sons of God. For the creation was subjected to futility, not willingly, but because of him who subjected it, in hope that the creation itself will be set free from its bondage to corruption and obtain the freedom of the glory of the children of God. For we know that the whole creation has been groaning together in the pains of childbirth until now. (Rom. 8:19–22 ESV)

Rocks, trees, meadows, even your neighbor's dog—nothing is exempt from Paul's diagnosis. Nothing is as it should be: disease, tsunamis, hurricanes, perverts, greed, earthquakes, and yes, the day when nothing seems to go your way. There is an intense realism in the biblical portrait of life. Pain and suffering do not surprise God; we do not need to deny them.

The appropriate response to life in this world *is* grief and pain. In fact, nowhere in the Bible do we find God sanctioning a "suck it up and deal with it" posture toward pain. Consider the life of Job again. He had everything going for him. He had land, wealth, a successful business, a woman at his side, and ten great kids. Job lived the good life. Then the nightmare struck. After being told that all of his ten children had died, Job's response was not a temperate one:

> Then Job arose and tore his robe and shaved his head and fell on the ground and worshiped. And he said, "Naked I came from my mother's womb, and naked shall I return. The LORD gave, and the LORD has taken away; blessed be the name of the LORD."
>
> In all this Job did not sin or charge God with wrong. (Job 1:20–22 ESV)

Note that God did not condemn Job's emotional outburst! It's not as if God saw Job's anguish and said, "Come on, Job! Get ahold of yourself and toughen up, man, seriously? Don't you know that I'm God and all of this has been done for a reason? And it's a darn good reason too, so just quit with the whining!"

Instead, what does the Bible say?

"In all this, Job did not sin."

Job's unraveling wasn't wrong or sinful; rather, it was emotionally realistic.

The emotional realism of the Bible took on a new urgency for me when my father was dying in late 2009 and early 2010. Before he died, he lived in the intensive care unit for about five months, following liver transplant surgery. I remember going to see him in the hospital one night after a meeting at church. It was the first time I had been to see him after his surgery. And I walked into the intensive care unit and burst into tears—it was almost uncontrollable. There were tubes coming out of every part of his body; he was bloated; he was discolored; I had never physically seen my father look like this. He looked dead. It was devastating. Job's friends must have had an image in their minds of what their friend looked like and who he was. Then they saw him, and even from a distance they didn't recognize him. And when they finally recognized him and saw how disfigured and undone he was, they wept aloud, just like me in that hospital room.

The good news here is that Christianity is in no way a stoic faith. It fundamentally rejects the "stiff upper lip" school of thought. Unfortunately, some Christians are guilty of throwing out an equivalent sentiment when they play the "God is sovereign" card as a way to trump every evil that comes your way.

"Sure, trouble will come, but don't cry," says the Sovereignty Card Stoic. "Don't allow yourself to feel deep, painful emotions. After all, God is in complete control. If you show lack of self-control, you must not be living in faith."

The less traditional version of this religious stoicism is what is known as the prosperity gospel. Taken to the extreme, the prosperity worldview essentially makes the experience of brokenness and pain the fault of the sufferer because of the inability to muster enough personal faith. I've actually heard people say that we tie God's hands when we don't simply reach out in faith and take what He promised. Whether it's money, health, or success, we suffer in life because we haven't exercised our faith.

If you have heard—or are hearing—these kinds of things, someone is lying to you. Such responses to pain and suffering are utter folly. This is not a biblically faithful way to respond to suffering, and neither does God treat it that way. According to Romans 8, the fallenness of humankind has cosmic ramifications. We live amid devastating brokenness, and the cure for this is nothing less than Jesus dying on the cross for sinners like you and me.

Today, God invites you to grieve your pains and losses and to acknowledge that the world is seriously broken. This does not mean casting yourself as the self-pitying victim of circumstances beyond your control, or indulging in entitlement when it comes to God and your fellow sufferers. Make no mistake, we are all both victims *and* victimizers. Just as everyone suffers, no one is innocent of causing suffering. This simply means we face up to the reality of our own suffering and need, which is 100 percent.

HONESTY AS THE DOORWAY TO GRACE

You might ask if all this talk is a bit morose. What is the point of harping on such negativity? Where is the hope? I'll explain with a conversion story from Sean Norris, who described a life-altering interaction with a professor:

> "We are *all* sufferers under our sin." It cut straight through me. I almost didn't believe him. It was the first time that someone had validated the pain that I had experienced as a sinner. It was the first time I felt truly addressed. Here I was, a western, white, suburban, Christian male. According to the Christianity of my upbringing, I had never *really* suffered in my life. I had never experienced starvation or extreme poverty. I had not been persecuted for my faith. I had not been harassed or wrongfully imprisoned, and so on. But in a single swipe, my teacher dismissed all of that. He told us to stop comparing ourselves to others, stop comparing ourselves to people in the third world, to people who are "really suffering." He leveled the playing field and destroyed the categories and false hierarchies I had put myself in. Instead, he told us the truth. The only

> point of comparison that truly mattered was the perfect demand of the law. In that light, there was no exception, we were all condemned and, as a result, we all had the same need ... the need for grace. I was pointed back to Jesus Christ and His cross, the one who knows our suffering and chose to suffer it once and for all, so that our stories would cease to be about guilt and shame and would become about forgiveness and freedom. I learned that day that the gospel was for me, and it changed my life forever. (emphasis original)[10]

God is not interested in what you think you *should* be or feel. He is not interested in the narrative you construct for yourself, or that others construct for you. He may even use suffering to deconstruct that narrative. Rather, He is interested in you, the you who suffers, the you who inflicts suffering on others, the you who hides, the you who has bad days (and good ones). And He meets you where you are. Jesus is not the man at the top of the stairs; He is the man at the bottom, the friend of sinners, the savior of those in need of one. Which is all of us, all of the time, praise be to God!

NOTES

1. Mary Karr, interview by Dean Nelson, Writer's Symposium by the Sea Sponsored by Point Loma Nazarene University,

Februaray 16, 2011, accessed June 4, 2012, www.youtube.com/watch?v=t9qYvJF7qx0&.

2. Larry Crab, *Shattered Dreams: God's Unexpected Path to Joy* (Colorado Springs, CO: WaterBrook: 2001), 65.
3. Robert Mankoff, "Look, I can't promise I'll change, but I can promise I'll pretend to change," *New Yorker*, August 2, 1999, cartoon.
4. Sinclair Ferguson, quoted in "Gospel Centered Life," *Monergism*, accessed June 15, 2012, http://www.monergism.com/monthly_focus/gospel_centered_life.php.
5. Stephen Marche, "Is Facebook Making Us Lonely?," *Atlantic*, May 2012, accessed June 14, 2012, http://www.theatlantic.com/magazine/archive/1969/12/is-facebook-making-us-lonely/8930/.
6. Sherry Turkle, *Alone Together: Why We Expect More from Technology and Less from Each Other,* quoted in Michiko Kakutani, "'Friends' without a Personal Touch," *New York Times,* February 21, 2011, accessed June 14, 2012, http://www.nytimes.com/2011/02/22/books/22book.html.
7. Hui-Tzu Grace Chou and Nicholas Edge, "'They Are Happier and Having Better Lives than I Am': The Impact of Using Facebook on Perceptions of Others' Lives," *Cyberpsychology, Behavior, and Social Networking* 15 (February 2012): 117–21, doi:10.1089/cyber.2011.0324.
8. Cornelius Plantinga Jr., *Not the Way It's Supposed to Be: A Breviary of Sin* (Grand Rapids, MI: Eerdmans, 1995), 10.

9. In Romans 8:18, Paul made an amazing claim: "For I consider that the sufferings of this present time are not worth comparing with the glory that is to be revealed to us" (ESV). About this passage, Justin and Lindsey Holcomb wrote: "He says your current sufferings will seem slight when compared to the glory that will be revealed. This is not to deny suffering. Paul concedes that suffering is painfully real. But in comparison to glory, suffering looks different because it is dwarfed by the grandeur of glory awaiting believers. It is important to see that rather than minimizing suffering, Paul is actually maximizing glory" (Justin S. Holcomb and Lindsey A. Holcomb, *Rid of My Disgrace* [Wheaton, IL: Crossway, 2011], 151).
10. Sean Norris, "Grace for Everyone," *Mockingbird*, May 24, 2011, accessed June 14, 2012, http://www.mbird.com/2011/05/grace-for-everyone/.

PART II:

CONFRONTING SUFFERING

Many and various are the things to which a man may feel himself drawn, but one thing there is to which no man ever felt himself drawn in any way, that is, to suffering and humiliation. This we men think we ought to shun as far as possible, and in any case that we must be compelled to it.

—Søren Kierkegaard, *The Prayers of Kierkegaard*

CHAPTER 4

MORALIZING SUFFERING

Good people get good stuff. Bad people get bad stuff. Or as the Beatles sang with their last gasp on *Abbey Road*, "In the end, the love you take is equal to the love you make."[1]

Now I love John, Paul, George, and Ringo, but I take issue with them here, and I know I am in the minority. After all, the world runs on retribution. "This for that" comes as naturally to us as breathing. While no one can deny that our actions have consequences—that if you put your finger in a light socket you will "reap" a shock—we do God (and ourselves!) a great disservice when we project this false schema onto Him. That is, when we moralize our suffering and that of others. The lab test results come back positive, and we interpret it as some sort of punishment. Or your loved ones interpret it that way. Your marriage falls apart, and you assume God is meting out His judgment on your indiscretions. Most of us—not all, I'm afraid—would stop short of blaming the citizens of New Orleans for the devastation of Hurricane Katrina, but that doesn't mean we don't moralize our suffering in other, more subtle ways.

Christians believe that Jesus severed the link between suffering and deserving once for all on Calvary. God put the ledgers away and settled the accounts. But when you and I insist on that all-too-comfortable paradigm of cosmic score keeping, we stop talking about Christianity and in fact adopt a Westernized form of Hinduism. We are talking about karma. If you are a bad person and things are going well for you, it is only a matter of time before karma catches up with you and "you get yours." If you are good person, the inverse is true: just be patient and your good deeds will come back to you. This is a simplification of the complex Hindu understanding of history as determined by the past lives of others: that we are all stuck in an eternal cycle of suffering perpetuated by reincarnation.

Westerners are understandably reticent to embrace the notion that the universe is paying us back for a prior life of boozing, spousal abuse, or tax evasion. We believe in the inherent goodness of human beings, after all! We prefer to keep the cycle within the confines of a single life. But the appeal of this perspective should be fairly obvious: no one gets away with anything. If someone harmed you, she will suffer. If you do good, you will have a good life. Karma puts us in control. The problem in this worldview comes, as it always does, when we flip it around. If you are suffering, you have done something to merit it. Pain is proof.

No doubt many of us would object to the accusation that we share or agree with such a mind-set. *That's simplistic nonsense*, we might think. *No one with any education or experience would ever hold to such a juvenile relational bartering system.* But hold on for a moment. Think about the last fight you had with your significant other—was there an element of deserving tucked into the conflict? "You hurt me, so now I'll hurt you"?

I can't tell you how much self-abuse I've come across in my years of ministry that had some element of inward-directed retribution at its core: the teenage girl who punishes herself by cutting her arms; or men who sleep around to prove that they deserve the contempt of their wives. If we cling to quid pro quo when dealing with others and ourselves, why wouldn't we project it onto God (or the universe)? We are all helpless moralizers, especially when it comes to suffering.

In this chapter we will look briefly at a few of the different ways this method makes sense of suffering, and how the gospel of Jesus Christ ultimately defies all such attempts.

THE PROSPERITY ANTIGOSPEL

If you know or have heard about American megachurches, you've likely heard the term "prosperity gospel." While it does not refer to a formalized school of theology, there are certainly a few broad strands of thought that characterize this teaching.

First, God wants to bless you and me. He is deeply concerned with both our personal happiness and our personal obedience to His Law. Sounds good, right? It's not hard to figure out why this teaching has such appeal.

Second, in His Word, He revealed how we can claim the tangible rewards that He promised us (success, riches, relationships).

Third, the way to attain and experience the prosperity that God wants for you is by exercising your faith: naming and claiming, if you will. Furthermore, if you experience suffering in some way, it's a result of either a lack of faith or some hidden sin. Perhaps you erected some barrier that keeps God from working in your life. You do not believe enough, or you do not live well enough. In all cases, the emphasis is firmly on the believer and his or her abilities (or lack thereof).

As an aside, whenever our ears pick up an "if-then" statement, we can reliably assume we are in the arena of the law. "If you want to live, then you will obey the Lord's commands." "If you meet my standard of (beauty, wealth, intelligence), then I'll love you." The gospel, on the other hand, says, "I'll love you despite the fact that you may not meet My standards or obey My commands."

Grace fundamentally rejects the circularity of karma.

In extreme prosperity theology, words themselves are containers of power—both positive and negative. When it comes to sickness and disease, the power of negative words causes suffering in the life of the believer. Words are also containers of faith (hence the phrase "word of faith"), and since God's Word cannot be confounded, all believers must do to live victoriously is simply speak words of faith into their circumstances, and they will receive the healing and prosperity that God promises. But as Phillip Cary has said, we are beginning to believe our own advertisements:

> Like every consumer product, the new evangelical theology is always advertising itself—and

> advertising is always about how great it is to experience the product that's being advertised. No advertiser ever lets on that there's deep suffering in the world and that it might be your job to participate in it. And so the promises of Christ, which are for our comfort and encouragement, become advertising slogans that we have to live up to in order to keep up our image as Christians—as if to say, "Look at me. I'm living the victorious Christian life, as advertised!" Our Lord promises abundant life (John 10:10), so if your life doesn't look very abundant these days, you have to wonder what's wrong with you.[2]

Sadly, this "new evangelical theology"—the prosperity gospel—has left a legacy of spiritual wreckage in the lives of countless believers who simply desired to love and obey God.[3] The prosperity gospel does not answer why bad things happen; it merely encourages us to focus on how to live in the present. It tells us that God is a good God, who gives only good things to His children. Which is about as classic a half-truth as you could possibly find.

Unfortunately, Christians are never, ever promised in the Bible that God will rescue us from our suffering—*never*. It is extremely difficult to study the book of Job or the letters of Paul and still believe in the teachings of the prosperity theology.

In fact, the Bible is replete with examples of faithful men and women who suffer, Jesus being the most obvious example. The Christian tradition is full of those who have suffered death and persecution as a result of their faith and, in some cases, for no discernible reason whatsoever. Roman Catholics call them saints! C. S. Lewis put it more eloquently than I ever could: "We were … promised sufferings. They were part of the programme. We were even told 'Blessed are they that mourn.'"[4]

As much as we might wish it weren't so, biblical faith ultimately eschews such conditionality. You simply cannot look at the cross and see the suffering of Jesus on behalf of rebellious sinners like you and me without also accepting that God sometimes ordains pain. This is not to say that suffering is *never* the result of something you or I have done, that it *can't* be related to some form of deserving. Rather, it just means that there is no longer a one-to-one correlation. In fact, there may not be any correlation at all!

So while the prosperity gospel pays lip service to the God of the Bible, it worships a God who waits for the suffering person to snap out of it and claim victory. In other words, it posits a God who is powerless to save sinners.

THE OPRAH-FICATION OF SUFFERING

Because the desire to moralize suffering is universal, there are plenty of nonreligious versions of this impulse. It can take slightly less straightforward forms, such as the gospel of self-transformation promoted in many books and on daytime talk shows.

Pop gurus like Oprah Winfrey espouse a sort of karma-flavored obsession with personal transformation that "repurposes" tragedy and pain as a conduit for self-improvement and personal gain. Her approach somehow manages to simultaneously moralize and minimize suffering.

In May 2011, the *New York Times* ran an insightful piece written by Mark Oppenheimer that aptly described the "Oprahfication" of suffering. Oppenheimer quoted Eva Illouz, the author of *Oprah Winfrey and the Glamour of Misery*:

> Ms. Winfrey and her cadre of self-help experts treated suffering as something beneficial. Ms. Winfrey turned the black church's ethos of self-reliance in the face of suffering into an exaltation of suffering itself. By making all experiences of suffering into occasions to improve oneself … Oprah ends up—absurdly—making suffering into a desirable experience.[5]

In other words, suffering—especially the traumatic kind—becomes a blessed opportunity to learn from your pain and reemerge on the other side a better and stronger person. Suffering as a strangely glamorous way to improve yourself may sound absurd, but it's not as far-fetched as one might think. Who doesn't want their suffering to have a redemptive purpose? While on the surface Oprah's "turning toward suffering" tactics may sound deceptively like a theology of the cross, they are actually a narcissistic version of the theology of glory, which seeks to "see through" or minimize painful circumstances.

Considerably more worrying is the implication that if a sufferer is not able to transcend her situation and make lemonade out of lemons, she has only herself to blame. Oppenheimer goes on to quote Kathryn Lofton, who said that *The Oprah Winfrey Show* made viewers feel that they constantly had to "sculpt their best lives." He concluded, though, that "in her religious exuberance Ms. Winfrey gave people some badly broken tools."[6]

Oprah's therapeutic religion attempts to rationalize suffering by generalizing it for common human experience.[7] This shared "community" functions as a sort of support group, urging members to overcome their own suffering, quite the opposite of twelve-step programs like Alcoholics Anonymous.

Now, far be it from me to pick on Ms. Winfrey unfairly, or turn her into a scapegoat for what is ultimately a universal human impulse. Certainly the commiseration and honesty about suffering that she encourages are commendable. And Lord knows there are much worse things going on in the world. The issue here is not Ms. Winfrey herself, or even her public persona. No, the issue has more to do with how she championed the self-transformation craze in a way that borrows liberally from the Christianity of her youth, and therefore led countless sufferers down the rabbit hole. Take Oprah's Book Club, for example. One of the most distinctive elements of each of the selected books is this basic plotline: living through and making sense of loss, evil, and the resulting disintegration of self. In traditional tragic narratives, the plot progresses toward the final demise of the hero or heroine. Instead, Oprah's Book Club books give the tragedy away at the beginning, suggesting that "what draws the reader in is the question of how a character will cope with something already known to be awful."[8]

This may sound a bit familiar. The story of Job follows the same basic tragedy-first plotline. But, as we'll see later, there is a vast difference between the book of Job and the gospel of self-transformation. If anything, the gospel of self-transformation bears an uncanny resemblance to the mentality of Job's friends, who endlessly berate him to confess his "secret sin." They believe the key to his situation is in his hands! "Good people," in their estimation, simply don't suffer the way Job did. Job must have done *something* to deserve such tribulation.

Our obsession with the idea of karma, whatever we call it, hasn't diminished since the time of the Old Testament. Today we live in a culture where instead of people having done something to deserve their troubles, we all seem to believe that people deserve something *for* their troubles. If bad things happen to good people, then they deserve more good stuff! No one typifies this mentality (and its pitfalls) more than America's favorite television "loser," Mr. George Costanza.

> George: So he's keeping the apartment. He doesn't deserve it, though! Even if he did suffer, that was, like, 40 years ago! What has he been doing lately?! I've been suffering for the past 30 years up to and including yesterday!

> Jerry: You know, if this tenant board is so impressed with suffering, maybe you should tell them the "Astonishing Tales of Costanza."
>
> George: (Interested) I should!
>
> Jerry: I mean, your body of work in this field is unparalleled.
>
> George: I could go bumper to bumper with any one else on this planet!
>
> Jerry: You're the man![9]

You might recognize this dialogue from *Seinfeld*. In the episode in question ("The Andrea Doria"), someone promises the long-suffering George Costanza a new apartment in his building. But then a fellow tenant, who happens to be a survivor of the famous *Andrea Doria* shipwreck, voices a claim, at which point George's offer is revoked. According to the tenant association, suffering earns a person a higher place on the list and, thus, a greater reward. George, who in classic biblical (and comedic) fashion, is his own worst enemy *par excellence*, both the cause and the victim of an absurd amount of suffering throughout the show's run, decides to plead his own case. He runs through a rudimentary list of his misadventures, and it leaves the board in tears:

> In closing, these stories have not been embellished, because—they need no embellishment. They are simply, horrifyingly, the story of my life

> as a short, stocky, slow witted bald man. (Gets up) Thank you.... Oh, also ... my fianc[é]e died from licking toxic envelopes that I picked out.[10]

This is a brilliant and hilarious characterization of how many of us confront suffering. Rather than face the underlying reasons for our distress (or look outside of ourselves for some relief), we attempt to leverage our pain for reward. Suffering becomes another way to justify ourselves, another form of works righteousness—a competition just as grueling as the obedience one.

For George, and many of us, victimhood becomes a tool of entitlement, a method for cracking the code of karma. But it doesn't work. Not for George (the apartment ends up going to someone who bribes the landlord), and not for us. On the show, George's stubborn refusal to give up makes for some inspired humor. For those of us who live our lives off the soundstage, however, this is no laughing matter.

THE TRAGEDY OF THE ME-GOSPEL AND SELF-TRANSFORMATION

Perhaps you or someone close to you is suffering, and some of this seems like an irrelevant or even mean-spirited exercise. I can assure you, compassion for fellow sufferers is the only reason I included it here.

Let me explain.

First, I offer a word of caution against dismissing the gospel of prosperity and self-transformation as something found only on daytime television or in the Astrodome. Unfortunately, an embarrassing number of evangelical churches toe essentially the same line as Oprah. Don't believe me? Again, think about the last testimony you heard from a Christian, where the newly (or not so newly) converted shared at length about his or her life of debauchery only to sneak in a quick shout-out at the end to good old G-O-D for making the transformation possible. In many cases, these testimonies are fueled by new-convert zeal and should be applauded. But sometimes I wonder if the reason we love these stories is because they appeal to our inner narcissism and do-it-yourself-ism.

Whether a person's starting point is religious or not, the examples above show our universal propensity to look inward for salvation. A karmic system is one we can (theoretically) influence and control, if only we try hard enough. Sure, you'll need some good advice and tips along the way. But the basic message is this: be your own savior.[11] And at the risk of sounding critical of public Christian testimonies, if we're not careful, we end up inverting what is most important. *God* is the one to be praised, not our *transformation*.[12]

What happens to those who subscribe to the transformational power of suffering who are themselves not transformed? Who never experience reward? Whose depression seems to grow worse with the years rather than better? Whose personality follows the same trajectory? Does God not care about them? Did He not die for our aging parents who seem to lose more of their faculties every year rather than improve them? The false gospel of self-fueled transformation is a glory-road narrative that inflicts spiritual pain on those who most need the comfort of the risen Christ.

THE TWOFOLD CRUELTY OF GLORY THEOLOGY

When it comes to the theology of glory, regardless of the form it takes, there are only two possible interpretations of tragedy. One, God is not who He says He is and is in fact a masochist who enjoys inflicting pain. After all, people still die prematurely of debilitating diseases despite a deep faith in Christ. Babies are born with birth defects through no fault of their own, and natural disasters still claim the lives of good-intentioned, faithful believers. If you subscribe to a human-centered theology with personal progress as its focal point, you face a cruel God who holds out the carrot of the good life but instead delivers the opposite. In this schema, we experience only as much peace or joy as we can carve out ourselves—God is essentially an obstacle to our well-being. The second interpretation is that God is a brutally tough but relatively powerless taskmaster who demands that we do more and try harder to break through to the "second blessing" and the "abundant life." He is dependent on us, not vice versa.

Both of these flawed conceptions of God share a common theme: if there's any rescue to be had in difficult times, *it's up to me.* Jesus has done His part. He'll meet me halfway, but the rest is my responsibility. So buck up, shut up, and get to work.

Glory-road theology buckles under the weight of suffering in this world. It is a false religion that burns us every time. Which is exactly what it does to Job when he hears it from his "friends." Indeed, under the guise of "counsel," they give him thirty-odd chapters of this despair-inducing mind-set, offering answers firmly ensconced within the prison of Why. "Job, we know how the world works," his friends say. "Good people are blessed, and bad people are cursed. That is *why* suffering happens. You are obviously being cursed, so what is it that you have done wrong? Show us the skeletons in your closet. Because God is just, there is no way He would allow you to suffer so profoundly unless you deserved it."

That's the moralistic presumption made by Job's friends: he is suffering as a direct result of bad behavior, or a particular sin.

Fortunately, the book of Job is far from the final word in the Bible on this method of dealing with suffering. In fact, Jesus Himself tackles the topic of karma head-on. In the ninth chapter of John, Jesus and His disciples come across a blind man.

His disciples asked him, "Rabbi, who sinned, this man or his parents, that he was born blind?"

> "Neither this man nor his parents sinned," said Jesus, "but this happened so that the works of God might be displayed in his life." (John 9:2–3)

I'm not sure how Jesus could be any clearer! Something else was going on in this man's suffering than a this-for-that retributive exchange. The man's affliction was not evidence of a curse or punishment. In fact, God was somehow present in it. The works of God displayed in infirmity and weakness, rather than health and strength? Is that a cross hanging around your neck? Perhaps it is no coincidence that the man who spoke these words would do more than voice them.

He would live and die them.

I'll close the chapter with an excerpt from the appropriately titled book *Beyond Deserving* by renowned child psychologist Dorothy Martyn:

> My own fascination with the truth that there is something very important beyond our deserving began some decades ago when I heard a sermon on the parable of the workers in the vineyard (Matt. 20:1–16), who all received the same pay from the master, though some had worked a long day, some a half-day, and some just a short part of a day.
>
> The unforgettable gift from that sermon was a new understanding that the major biblical message is about something that cannot be earned. In this parable, "fairness" and "merit" utterly disappear in an in-breaking of a powerful force that transcends "deserving" altogether.
>
> In my decades of working with children and families, the significance of this force has become incarnate before my eyes.... Love ... is authentic and effectual in proportion to

> the degree that it transcends the commonly assumed principle of the circular exchange, that is to say, "this for that." All true love is a stranger to that kind of thinking. The "justice" idea of reward according to what is deserved is replaced by the much more powerful force of noncontingent, compassionate alliance.... Such a stance is in fact derived from the way that God enters into human suffering with mercy, moving first with grace—not waiting for bad behavior to change—and with patience, that is to say, sustaining and accompanying the human being without coercion.[13]

Now *that* sounds like a woman whose body of work in this field is truly unparalleled.

NOTES

1. The Beatles, "The End," *Abbey Road* © 1969 George Martin.
2. Phillip Cary, *Good News for Anxious Christians* (Grand Rapids, MI: Brazos Press, 2010), 138.
3. For further reading on the error of Word of Faith teaching, see Hank Hanegraaff, *Christianity in Crisis* (Eugene, OR: Harvest House, 1997).
4. C. S. Lewis, *A Grief Observed* (London: Faber, 1961), 48.
5. Mark Oppenheimer, "The Church of Oprah Winfrey and a Theology of Suffering," *New York Times,* May 27, 2011,

accessed June 5, 2012, http://www.nytimes.com/2011/05/28/us/28beliefs.html.

6. Oppenheimer, "The Church of Oprah Winfrey."
7. In one sense, it is a bit odd that *The Oprah Winfrey Show* devoted so much time to narratives of suffering. Yet, as Eva Illouz explained, "Oprah Winfrey has become an international and a mighty (western) symbol, because she offers a new cultural form through which to present and process suffering generated by the 'chaos' of intimate social relationships, one of the major cultural features of the late modern era. Oprah Winfrey shows us how to cope with chaos by offering a rationalized view of the self, inspired by the language of therapy, to manage and change the self. *The Oprah Winfrey Show* is a popular cultural form that makes sense of suffering at a time when psychic pain has become a permanent feature of our polities and when, simultaneously, so much in our culture presumes that well-being and happiness depend on successful self-management." That is to say, Oprah's focus on suffering is powerful only because she offers a form of identity that purports to overcome suffering. It is important to note, however, that Oprah's discussion of suffering is often disconnected from any talk of suffering as pertaining to religion. "For example, when discussing her own life or that of her guests, Oprah Winfrey frequently uses the language of suffering and pain. This alerts us that 'suffering' is a central cultural code we can use to probe the meaning of her cultural enterprise. But this does not mean

that Oprah is aware of the relation that the contemporary language of suffering may (or may not) bear to the cultural tradition of Christianity, the political lexicon of rights, or therapeutic discourse" (Eva Illouz, *Oprah Winfrey and the Glamour of Misery: An Essay on Popular Culture* [New York: Columbia University Press, 2003], 5, 20).

8. "What makes the characters of these novels heroines is not that they are looking for love or success or sexual liberation, but simply and almost exclusively the fact that they face a severe threat to their identity caused by the plagues publicized in the present time (AIDS, domestic violence, mental retardation, abuse, rape, divorce, betrayal, etc.) and that, as a consequence, they reexamine the meaning of their self and usually find a new one" (Illouz, *Oprah Winfrey*, 108–9).
9. "The Andrea Doria," *Seinfeld*, season 8, episode 10, NBC, aired December 19, 1996, script accessed June 5, 2012, http://www.seinology.com/scripts/script-144.shtml.
10. "The Andrea Doria," *Seinfeld*.
11. Kathryn Lofton, *Oprah: The Gospel of an Icon* (Berkeley: University of California Press, 2011), 5. Lofton, quoting Oprah on the subject of self-transformation: "'Originally our goal was to uplift, enlighten, encourage, and entertain through the medium of television,' Winfrey explained. 'Now our mission … is to use television to transform people's lives, to make viewers see themselves differently, and to bring happiness and a sense of fulfillment into every home.' To transform, to bring happiness, to create a 'sense'

of fulfillment: these are callings of the highest order. 'I am talking about each individual having her or his own inner revolution,' Winfrey explained. 'I am talking about each individual coming to the awareness that, "I am Creation's son. I am Creation's daughter. I am more than my physical self. I am more than this job that I do. I am more than the external definitions I have given myself.... Those roles are all extensions of who I define myself to be, but ultimately I am Spirit come from the greatest Spirit. I am Spirit"'" (Lofton, 107–8).

12. Mark Galli, "Are We Transformed Yet?," *Christianity Today*, February 4, 2010, accessed June 5, 2012, http://www.christianitytoday.com/ct/2010/februaryweb-only/15-41.0.html?start=1.
13. Dorothy Martyn, *Beyond Deserving: Children, Parents, and Responsibility Revisited* (Grand Rapids, MI: Eerdmans, 2007), xiv–xv, 126.

CHAPTER 5

MINIMIZING SUFFERING

It is ironic that one of the most beautiful and encouraging verses in the Bible is also one of the most dangerous. You probably know which one I'm talking about. "And we know that in all things God works for the good of those who love him, who have been called according to his purpose" (Rom. 8:28).

I've witnessed that verse misused more than any other. And I know I have been guilty of misusing it myself. Maybe you've heard it thrown out in a small-group setting, maybe in a casual discussion. Inevitably someone has just shared a painful story about what she's going through or has gone through. We don't know what to say—the predicament is a sad one. It goes beyond the normal categories and struggles. It's awkward. We want to help, perhaps, but we also want the moment to end. Or maybe we are just focused on saying the "right" thing, the faithful thing. Make no mistake, in this context, Romans 8:28 can be a bona fide conversation stopper. A spiritual "shut up," if you will. And lest we think only Christians are prone to such insensitivity, the secular translation, "Don't worry; it'll all work out," is no less ubiquitous. This is classic minimization, just as ill advised a way of dealing with suffering as moralization and, unfortunately, no less common.

Minimization involves any attempt to downplay or reduce the extent and nature of pain. Any rhetorical or spiritual device that underestimates the seriousness of suffering essentially minimizes it. Quick fixes are inevitably minimizing tactics. Platitudes are minimizing tactics. If moralization reduces suffering to a moral or spiritual issue, minimization makes similar reductions. For example, when doctors reduce suffering to a matter of medication or chemistry, or psychologists to one's dysfunctional upbringing (which is not to say those things can't be factors). In fact, naturalistic or materialistic outlooks are especially susceptible to minimization.

Whether suffering is approached through the eyes of faith or not, the God of the Bible never reduces or compartmentalizes suffering—*ever*. The problems of life are large and complex; pat answers are not only inaccurate but also unkind. In this chapter, we'll consider a few forms this approach takes, both secular and religious, from neuroscience and philosophy to religious ones in prosperity gospel and run-of-the-mill glory-road theology.

RELIGIOUS MINIMIZING

In his book *Shattered Dreams*, Larry Crabb related the experience of a man who suffered an enormous loss. Crabb described the man's friends as concerned and supportive, sending books on handling grief, spending time with him both in prayer and on the golf course, etc. Several friends sent letters expressing their love, and a few included verses from the Bible they said had been impressed on them by the Lord.

> When his friends called or came to visit, the first question after a quick greeting was always "How are you doing?"
>
> He hated the question the first time he heard it and hated it more each time he heard it again. He knew the "right" answer, the one his friends were hoping to hear, the one that had more to do with relieving their concern than with expressing his own heart. The hoped-for answer could be expressed in many ways, but its message was always the same. "It's hard, but I'm okay, or at least I'm getting there."
>
> … His words [had] their intended effect. The questioner smiled with relief and said, "I'm really glad. Not surprised though. Lots of us have been praying." … As the struggling man listened to his friend, he felt a tidal wave of intense loneliness sweep over him. He returned the smile but his soul shriveled behind a familiar wall that left him lifeless, more desperate and alone than before.[1]

As the story illustrates, when the bottom falls out of our lives, we don't necessarily find it comforting when people try to cheer us up. No matter how well intended, such overtures create pressure that adds to our distress. Not only are we suffering, but we now feel bad about how we make those around us feel or, at least, about the disconnect between where they would like us to be and where we actually are.

This is classic glory-road theology. As we have discussed, a theology of glory sees God at work in the victories of life rather than the defeats. So the role of the Christian is to help her fellow believers get back on "the glory road" when they suffer setbacks. In tragedy, the theologian of glory will incessantly look for some measure of improvement on which to hang her hope, and if not, she will attempt to be the agent of improvement herself. The underlying assumption is that if the Holy Spirit is working, the sufferer would feel better. One theologian described the reality this way:

> Although God does sometimes give the feeling of "a kind of peace with God", and does communicate with his people in a personal and guiding way, God's primary way of doing so is through "negative" experiences, in which our guilt and the true limits of our supposed autonomy are made manifest. Through these experiences of the Spirit, we die to ourselves again and again, in such a way as to pave the way for transformation and new life.[2]

On a basic pastoral or relational level, a theology of the cross allows us to love and serve a suffering person independent of whether or not, or how fast, he is healing. We can walk with these people in their present pain, as opposed to impatiently focusing on their future health.

God is *right* there, not somewhere else.

As we touched on in the last chapter, prosperity theology also tends to minimize suffering. Rather than embrace a realistic outlook on the inevitability of suffering, the prosperity gospel speaks continually about the (nonsuffering) happiness that God apparently has in store for those who choose to live in the blessing of His perfect plan. No matter our past sufferings—"setbacks" is the euphemism prosperity preachers prefer—we are told that we can't allow our past to determine our future.

Even when we've lived through abusive situations, we don't want to make the mistake of inhibiting a great future God may have in store by dwelling on the past. Regardless of what happened, or who harmed us, we can't allow ourselves to accept the pain as possibly part of God's work in our life. What's done is done. We are told to let the past be the past and to move on. We may suffer setbacks, but, we're told, we're not alone. Many good people just like us have experienced the same thing. Needless to say, there is little about this outlook that would give even an inkling of hope to the sufferer. These preachers are often kind-hearted, compelling speakers, but the delivery and message are at odds with one another. In effect, sermons become pep talks that encourage us to quit our whining and buck up. Minimization!

SCIENTISM AND SUFFERING

"Neuroscience" is a buzzword these days, and for good reason. It seems like almost every week a new study comes out, shedding light on some new area of brain function. Perhaps most surprising is the degree to which many of these studies vindicate biblical understandings of human nature. For example, neuroscience confirms the idea that you and I are often at the mercy of forces beyond our control, that we are fundamentally self-oriented in a way that often works against us, that our hearts (emotions) tend to inform our heads (thoughts), rather than vice versa. The list goes on. And in fact, contrary to what you might think, the more we learn about the brain, the more awe inducing God's creation becomes—*not less*.

One area of life, however, where science offers few answers is the area of suffering. In fact, the dominant minimizing force in our culture often seems to be the voice from the laboratory. In 2010, the *New York Times* published a story titled "Depression's Upside,"[3] which tried to convince an unsuspecting public that depression serves a helpful purpose, that ruminating on our troubles allows us to develop better problem-solving skills.

A year later, *Wired* magazine ran a story about the benefits of anger, taking Steve Jobs as their primary example.[4] People are more creative when they're upset, we found out. Then, a few months afterward, *Time* magazine ran a cover feature titled "Anxiety: Friend or Foe?,"[5] asserting that anxiety can sharpen our senses when we need them most. No doubt these studies have some basis and merit—the problem comes when the minimizing impulse hijacks the interpretation process. And clearly, it was having a field day! Just like Oprah turning someone's personal suffering into a means of self-improvement, the researchers systematically took three of the most painful emotional afflictions a person can withstand and called them good, exonerating suffering in a particularly unconvincing way.

Behind most of these studies lies the conviction that if something has survived in nature over the eons, it must have a positive purpose. It must be good. This is what some pundits call "scientism." Taken to its *Lion King*/"Circle of Life" conclusion, you might as well say that "death is a natural part of life." Just see where that gets you when your neighbor's son develops a brain tumor at the age of sixteen.

Still, Christians fundamentally reject the idea that nature is always good. There are good elements of it, of course, but nothing has remained unsullied by the fall. "The whole creation groans," as we mentioned a few chapters ago. One commentator, another scientist, wisely noted that "nature offers us cancer, infections and heart disease."[6]

I might add that the minimizing approach to suffering is also a gift of nature! Truly, there is something almost manic about the secular crusade to validate the goodness of everything. Depression is soul crushing. Anxiety is the opposite of faith. Anger is the father of murder. And claiming a possible benefit says nothing about the essential awfulness of these things. If anything, it denies the full extent of a sufferer's pain and, therefore, his or her need. No, thank you!

NIHILISM AND SUFFERING

Of all the non-Christian belief systems that have anything to say about the nature and extent of human suffering, none is as consistent as atheistic nihilism.

Nihilism does not have a rosy view of the human self like therapeutic religion, the prosperity gospel, or scientism. Instead, nihilism despairs of the human condition and recognizes there is nothing in the world that can rationalize, minimize, or end the existence of suffering. And since there is no God, there is nothing that can ultimately vanquish suffering. Despair and sorrow are the only appropriate responses. Rather than try to sweep the horrors of suffering under the rug, nihilism confronts suffering. In a godless universe, nihilism is certainly consistent, and therefore hopeless.

One philosopher described it this way:

> Nihilism is the belief that all values are baseless and that nothing can be known or communicated. It is often associated with extreme pessimism and a radical skepticism that condemns existence. A true nihilist would believe in nothing, have no loyalties, and no purpose other than, perhaps, an impulse to destroy.... In the 20th century, nihilistic themes—epistemological failure, value destruction, and cosmic purposelessness—have preoccupied artists, social critics, and philosophers. Mid-century, for example,

> the existentialists helped popularize tenets of nihilism in their attempts to blunt its destructive potential. By the end of the century, existential despair as a response to nihilism gave way to an attitude of indifference.[7]

While textbook philosophies may seem like the dark underbelly of academia, the hooks of nihilism have sunk themselves deep into our culture, as evidenced by such benign occurrences as a teenager being bored with two hundred cable TV channels.

Theologian Michael Horton said this:

> Today, however, a lot of young people really *are* nihilists. If for [Friedrich] Nietzsche truth was not discovered but made, for many today truth is not even made but passively worn like a dress, adopted from popular culture. Not really happy, but also not sad; not really loved, but also not deprived—in fact, pampered—a lot of us simply sit back and let the true Nietzschean masters of the previous generation entertain us, feeding us their images of the true, the good, and the beautiful.... We are "in charge," but of a life that seems often to lack any definite purpose or sense of destination. So people conform their bodies to the fashion magazines, their souls to the self-help fads, and then return to suburban anonymity

> to start all over the next day. This restless, reckless, Dionysian pursuit of physical and spiritual "makeovers" is its own form of suffering. The masters have become slaves after all. (emphasis original)[8]

This banal, consumeristic nothingness is likely not what Nietzsche had in mind when he conceived the idea of his superman, or *Übermensch*. Instead of defiantly spitting into the blackness of the void, we are more interested in a couple of cold beers, a few buddies, and SportsCenter. In other words, if I'm a victim of random chance in a meaningless universe, if at worst there is no God and at best God is absent and uncaring, let's eat, drink, and be merry, for tomorrow we die.

But wait! According to Nietzsche—and oddly, Oprah, too—human suffering is also the linchpin of human excellence. Aiming for any sort of happiness makes a person unworthy of Nietzsche's admiration. As he put it elsewhere: "Only great pain is the ultimate liberator of the spirit.... I doubt that such pain makes us 'better'; but I know that it makes us more profound."[9]

He certainly believed as much when it came to his own work. He wrote the following, hyperbolically, in *Ecce Homo*: "Amid the tortures that go with an uninterrupted three-day migraine and agonizing phlegm-wretching, I possessed a dialectician's clarity *par excellence*, and very cold-bloodedly thought through matters for which, in healthier states, I am not enough of a climber, not subtle, not *cold* enough" (emphasis original).[10] This may sound grandiose—the opposite of minimization—but it is a grandiose exercise in instrumentalization. That is, like Oprah, Nietzsche took suffering to a hoped-for end result, and made it a means to a potentially glorious end.

It's an interesting idea, but what about the suffering of the nongeniuses?

Another influential philosopher whose understanding of suffering led him to wrestle with nihilism was Albert Camus. For Camus, "the silence of the universe has led me to conclude that the world is without meaning."[11]

Yet Camus was not content to remain a nihilist. He fought to transcend it, to make meaning where there was none, which is a self-made law if ever there was one. "Camus had doubts about his own solution and premonitions that genuine meaning did in fact exist in God as understood by traditional Christianity. 'I am searching for something I do not have, something I'm not sure I can define,' he tells Mumma in their first encounter. The world is not rational, it does not fit human needs and desire. 'In a word, our very existence is absurd.' Suicide seems the only logical response."[12]

Good grief!

But he has a point, and it's not a minimal one. When the songwriter Leonard Cohen sang, "Give me Christ or give me Hiroshima,"[13] I think he was trying to say the same thing.

Minimalization seems like a cruel joke in the face of lived experience.

THE GOSPEL IS MAXIMAL

There is a tie that binds all of the above examples of minimalization. In fact, it is the same thread that runs through the moralizing approach as well. I am talking about Original Sin. I am talking about our universal, fatal love affair with control and law. If I can just recast suffering in a diminished role, then I will hurt less. Or conversely, if I just do the right thing or just obey enough, God will be pleased, and I will hurt less. Neither approach takes God into much consideration. He is a passive bystander at best in either scenario. And both approaches stand on the premise of you and me possessing power that we simply do not have.

Yet the knowledge of our limitations does not stop us from exhausting ourselves—indeed, from destroying ourselves—in our tireless attempts to grab the reins. The breadth of human impasse is the opposite of minimal. Yet as Paul Zahl wrote:

> An old joke is repeated year after year in the graffiti on public buildings. Someone writes for all to see, "Christ is the answer." After it someone has added, "But what is the question?" The addition is perceptive.… Is there a real problem to which the atonement of Jesus Christ offers a solution? What is irremediable about the human condition that it should require a death for healing to occur? The extreme nature of the solution, one person's death for the "salvation" of others, presupposes an extreme need on the part of the others.[14]

The cross makes a mockery of our attempts to defend and deliver ourselves. God provided a shocking remedy that both reveals and addresses the depth of our illness, our "sickness unto death."

Indeed, despite our efforts to contain, move past, or silence it, that ol' rugged cross stands tall, resolutely announcing that "in all things God works for the good of those who love him, who have been called according to his purpose." All things, Paul said, even misused Bible verses and the men and women who misuse them. Instead of diminishing our pain, then, these words proclaim the corresponding and overwhelming gratuity of our Redeemer.

Amen.

NOTES

1. Larry Crabb, *Shattered Dreams* (Colorado Springs, CO: WaterBrook, 2001), 122–23.
2. Simeon Zahl, "Reformation Pessimism or Pietist Personalism? The Problem of the Holy Spirit in Evangelical Theology" in *New Perspectives for Evangelical Theology*, ed. Tom Greggs (New York: Routledge, 2010), 89.
3. Jonah Lehrer, "Depression's Upside," *New York Times*, February 25, 2010, accessed June 5, 2012, http://www.nytimes.com/2010/02/28/magazine/28depression-t.html?pagewanted=1&em.

4. Jonah Lehrer, "The Creativity of Anger," *Wired*, August 29, 2011, accessed June 5, 2012, http://www.wired.com/wiredscience/2011/08/the-creativity-of-anger/.
5. Alice Park, "Anxiety: Friend or Foe?," *Time*, November 23, 2011, accessed June 5, 2012, http://healthland.time.com/2011/11/23/anxiety-friend-or-foe/.
6. Richard A. Friedman, "Depression Defies the Rush to Find an Evolutionary Upside," *New York Times*, January 16, 2012, accessed June 5, 2012, http://www.nytimes.com/2012/01/17/health/depression-defies-rush-to-find-evolutionary-upside.html?_r=1.
7. Alan Pratt, "Nihilism," *Internet Encyclopedia of Philosophy*, accessed June 5, 2012, http://www.iep.utm.edu/nihilism/.
8. Michael S. Horton, *A Place for Weakness* (Grand Rapids, MI: Zondervan, 2010), 138.
9. Friedrich Wilhelm Nietzsche, *The Portable Nietzsche*, ed. and trans. Walter Kaufmann (New York: Penguin 1954), Google eBook, 680–81.
10. Friedrich Wilhelm Nietzsche, *The Portable Nietzsche,* 657–58. According to Nietzsche, human suffering is, in a sense, a cultivator of human excellence. Yet, this does not mean that suffering has any intrinsic value. For him, aiming for any sort of happiness makes a person unworthy of admiration "because *suffering* is positively necessary for the cultivation of human excellence—which is the only thing, recall, that warrants admiration for Nietzsche. He writes, for example, that: 'The discipline of suffering, of great suffering—do

you not know that only *this* discipline has created all enhancements of man so far? That tension of the soul in unhappiness which cultivates its strength, its shudders face to face with great ruin, its inventiveness and courage in enduring, persevering, interpreting, and exploiting suffering, and whatever has been granted to it of profundity, secret, mask, spirit, cunning, greatness—was it not granted to it through suffering, through the discipline of great suffering?' Nietzsche is not arguing here that … suffering is really *intrinsically* valuable.… The value of suffering, according to Nietzsche, is only extrinsic: suffering—'great' suffering—is a prerequisite of any great human achievement" (emphasis original). (Brien Leiter, "Nietzsche's Moral and Political Philosophy," *Stanford Encyclopedia of Philosophy*, April 14, 2010, accessed June 5, 2012, http://plato.stanford.edu/entries/nietzsche-moral-political/).

11. Albert Camus, quoted in James W. Sire, "The CT Review: Camus the Christian?," *Christianity Today*, October 23, 2000, accessed June 5, 2012, http://www.christianitytoday.com/ct/2000/october23/39.121.html.
12. James W. Sire, "The CT Review: Camus the Christian?"
13. Leonard Cohen, "The Future," *The Future* © 1992 Columbia.
14. Paul Zahl, *Who Will Deliver Us?* (New York: Seabury Press, 1983), 9.

PART III:

SAVED BY SUFFERING

Do not fret over your heavy troubles, for they are the heralds of weighty mercies.

—Charles Spurgeon, *Morning by Morning*

CHAPTER 6

THE FREEDOM OF DEFEAT

I heard something on the radio recently that made me pull my car over to the side of the road. A young woman named Sara was telling the story of her family's very public fall from grace. She grew up in a privileged family—enormous house, beautiful clothes, expensive cars (and schools), and country club memberships. Everything in her world was very prim and proper. But Sara claimed that despite the excess that could be seen from the outside, on the inside, her home environment was one of constraint.

"Rules were very important," Sara said. "Etiquette, very important. And my dad's insane temper could be set off by the slightest offense. When I heard the Porsche rumble up the driveway every day when he came home, I would run into my room and hide. Because maybe today would be the day he found the candy wrapper in the sofa cushion.... It was all just all about avoiding awakening the bee's nest."[1]

Sara went on to describe the fateful day when her parents called a family meeting to tell the children that her father had done something very wrong and was going to have to pay. He had embezzled much of their money, it turned out, from a trust fund of one of his disabled clients. In other words, he stole it.

Her father, who was a prominent lawyer, wept on the couch as he confessed his wrongdoing to his children. The guilt-induced suffering had become too much to bear. He couldn't live with his wrongdoing any longer. "We're going to have to start over. We are going to rebuild our lives." Sara then shared how her father was disbarred from practicing law, how they had to sell their house and cars and move to the other side of town. Her mother went to work. The scandal made headlines. At school, kids teased Sara for being the daughter of a "bankrobber." And yet in that death—of security, wealth, achievement, identity, etc.—we find out that new life is born.

Sara described it this way:

> But my dad was instantly better.... He was happy. He chewed gum, which didn't happen before. And wasn't such an ... all the time."[2]

Commenting on this story, Ethan Richardson wrote,

> With less money, the family gave more. With less status, they imputed status upon those who had none. In becoming the judged, they relinquished

> their judgments. Downward mobility was now the name of the game: the formerly constrained household became a "free for all."… In being freed from their bondage to the law of progress and upward mobility, Sara's family was now able to live in the reality of downward-directed love.[3]

Wow.

Sara's story is a powerful testimony of how suffering can liberate us, a tangible echo of the theology of the cross. The suffering of Sara's father was self-inflicted, as much suffering is, but there was nothing minimal about it. There is zero sense that he viewed his crisis as an avenue for personal growth. And yet real transformation did happen! The disaster actually freed him from himself: from his attachment to his possessions (and affections), from his obsession with appearances, from his judgments of others, from his need to remain upwardly mobile, and the list goes on. Failure, it turns out, was his gateway to freedom. The very real fruit was a by-product of this man's repentance rather than its goal, the opposite of the Oprah-fied self-improvement approach, or the reward-centered prosperity gospel one. Interesting.

We have talked about the ubiquity and gravity of suffering. We have looked at some of the ways we avoid suffering, and some of the ways we deal with it that make it worse. Now it's time to explore what it means for suffering to make us free, as the subtitle of this book suggests. In other words, now it is time to unpack the hope and truth hinted at in Sara's account of glorious ruin.

LET'S GET SMALL

The world tells us in a thousand different ways that the bigger we become, the freer we will be. The richer, the more beautiful, and the more powerful we grow, the more security, liberty, and happiness we will experience. And yet, the gospel tells us just the opposite, that the smaller we become, the freer we will be. This may sound at first like bad news, but as we will see, it could not be better news!

In the Bible, slavery is equated with self-reliance. Self-dependence, the burden of depending on yourself and controlling your circumstances to ensure meaning and security, safety and significance—just like Sara's father before his breakdown. But as we know, the burden of self-determination is enormous. When your meaning, your significance, your security, your protection, your safety are all riding on you, it actually feels like slavery.

People seldom "choose" to embezzle money; they feel like they *have* to if they are to uphold whatever law they live under. That is, they equate their value with some attribute or ability—what others think of them, how much is in their bank account, their relative stature in their community—and without that attribute or ability, they cease to matter. There is no "them" without "that," and so they do whatever they can to ensure they don't lose it!

This is a burden we were never meant to bear, and yet after the fall, self-reliance became our default mode of operation. Mine as well as yours. You might even call it our inheritance. In our exile from Eden, we naturally tend toward self-reliance.

Fortunately, God does not leave us there. God wants to free us from ourselves, and there's nothing like suffering to show us that we need something bigger than our abilities and our strength and our explanations. There's nothing like suffering to remind us how not in control we actually are, how little power we ultimately have, and how much we ultimately need God. In other words, suffering reveals to us the things that ultimately matter, which also happen to be the warp and woof of Christianity: who we are and who God is.

In 1990, media mogul Ted Turner announced to an audience at the American Humanist Association that "Christianity is a religion for losers." Instead of humbly and heartily affirming Turner's sentiment and perhaps using it as a potential springboard for evangelism, the Christian community got angry. Even now, Turner's judgment causes some people to bristle.

But Turner was exactly right!

The gospel *is* for the defeated, not the dominant. But his self-righteous tone was 100 percent wrong. That is, he was saying something true about God, but his success had clearly buffered him from understanding himself honestly and accurately. In view of God's holiness, we are *all* losers (Rom. 3:23).

We are all sufferers.

We are all sinners.

The distinction between winners and losers is irrelevant when no one can claim victory.

I remember going to see my grandfather receive the Congressional Gold Medal in the Capitol Rotunda in

Washington, DC in 1996. If you have ever been in the Capitol Rotunda, you know that it is decorated with the images of dead men, many of whom are the forefathers of our country.

He got up there in front of the vice president, senators, and congressmen, and said so plainly, "You're all going to die." It's so simple. He said, "Just look around the room. The one thing that can be said about all these men is they're all dead; you're all going to die."

You're going to die.

There are no winners in this game, Mr. Turner.

Instead, the gospel is for those who have realized that they can't carry the weight of the world on their shoulders. Only when God drives us to the end of ourselves do we begin to see life in the gospel. Which is another way of saying that only those who stand in need of a savior will look for or recognize a savior. Fortunately, Christianity in its original, most authentic expression understands God chiefly as savior (and human beings chiefly as those in need of being saved).

This is where the distinction between the theology of glory and the theology of the cross comes in again:

> The theology of glory sees God everywhere, in glory and in power, and presumes to ascend self-confidently to God by means of experience, rational speculation, and merit. It is the religion of the natural man or woman. By contrast, the theology of the cross sees God only where God

> has revealed himself, particularly in the weakness and mercy of the suffering. Only when we learn to despair of ourselves, to suffer our own nakedness in God's holy presence, to renounce our righteousness and listen only to God's Word, are we enabled to recognize God as our Savior rather than our just judge and holy enemy. We rise up to God in pride, while God descends to us in humility. We look for God in powerful places; in health, wealth, and happiness; in perfect families and prosperous nations, but God is truly to be found in weak things of the world. In other words, we are talking about a theology for winners versus a theology for losers.[4]

Why then don't Christians proudly wear the loser badge? Our discomfort with Turner's comment betrays the glory-road theologian in all of us, the non-Christian corner of our disbelieving hearts. Yet Jesus claimed that He came for those who are sick (the losers who *know* they're losers), not those who are well.

I thought I'd always understood this. Then I became pastor of Coral Ridge Presbyterian Church in 2009, and everything changed.

COME DIE WITH ME

Some readers may be familiar with the Coral Ridge Presbyterian Church merger story, a story that I share in detail in my book

Jesus + Nothing = Everything. And while I hesitate to repeat it here, the truth is, I would not be speaking honestly about suffering if I didn't reference that painful experience.

In short, after pastor D. James Kennedy passed away, I was asked to be the lead preaching pastor at Coral Ridge, a well-established, nationally renowned church in Fort Lauderdale, Florida. These were big shoes to fill, and initially, I wasn't interested in the offer. But after much prayer and consideration, it was decided that our church, New City, should merge with the larger Coral Ridge.

Just after the merger decision had been made, I cast a vision for our future together in a message to the congregation, by saying:

> A gospel-saturated church is a church filled with people who give everything they have because they understand that in Christ they already have everything they need.… So, having been duly installed and charged, I invite all of you to spend your life dying with me.

Novelists might call it foreshadowing, but I can assure you, though we expected some bumps in the road during the transition, I never dreamed that those words would be born out so radically.

Soon after the decision, disgruntled Coral Ridge members began aggressively circulating a petition to remove me. Various people dug trenches, took positions, and began shelling one another.

Anyone who has spent much time in churches knows that they are not immune from internal conflict. In fact, it sometimes seems like they are prone to it. Such was the case here. The conflict escalated and brought out the worst in everyone; no one was innocent, least of all me. Yet the viciousness of the opposition shocked me. It was hurtful, to say the least, and before long I wanted badly to escape. For the first time in my life, people not only didn't like me, but they were actively hostile toward me. In hindsight I can see that it was the beginning, or you might say culmination, of a long, exhausting period during which God revealed to me the depth of my idolatry and sin. I'm not proud, though I am grateful, to say that despite having been in ministry for most of my adult life, it took this painful trial to teach me the true meaning of the cross.

First, however, God used the crucible of suffering to disillusion me about who I was. The pain cleared my vision, and once it was taken away, I realized just how much I'd been relying on the endorsement of others to make me feel like I mattered. I had turned personal validation into my primary source of meaning and value (what theologians call the basis of my self-justification), so that without it I was miserable and depressed. I had made something good—the approval and admiration of others—into an idol.

As if that weren't enough, I became frustrated with myself for not being as sturdy and unquestioning as I knew a man in my position should be. And the pressure I put on myself to exhibit strength and faithfulness only exposed my frailty and faithlessness all the more. What kind of Christian leader was *I*? How could *I* allow these circumstances to get *me* down the way they had? Where was *my* faith? Where was *my* trust in God?

Augustine of Hippo is usually credited with describing our fallen nature as *incurvatus in se* or "mankind turned inward." And sadly, somewhere along the line, my understanding of the Christian life had become terribly narcissistic. I was becoming completely preoccupied with how I was doing, if was learning everything I was supposed to be learning during this difficult season, whether I was doing it right or not, and taking my own spiritual pulse. You might say that my "inner lawyer" was working overtime.

I dwelled on my failures and brooded over my momentary successes. In short, I was spending way too much time thinking about me and what I needed to do, and far too little time thinking about Jesus and what He had already done for me. What I discovered was that the more I focused on my need to get better, the worse I actually got—the more neurotic and self-conscious and self-absorbed I became. And so God took me up on my unwitting invitation to the congregation and gave me the gift I never meant to ask for: He gave me the gift of suffering. God did not rescue me out of the pain; He rescued me through the pain!

Indeed, I had to learn the hard way (the only way?) that the gospel alone can free us from our addiction to being liked—that Jesus measured up for us so that we wouldn't have to live under the enslaving pressure of measuring up for others—including ourselves. I finally understood what Paul meant in Romans 10:4 when he wrote that Christ is the "end of the law." Because of Jesus's finished work for me, I already had the justification, approval, acceptance, security, freedom, affection, cleansing, new beginning, righteousness, and rescue I longed for. There was nothing left to prove or protect, no one to impress or appease. I could be okay with not being okay. I was freed from the burden of trying to control what other people thought about me, from the miserable, unquenchable pursuit to make something of myself. I was free to be honest, with others, with myself, and with God. Indeed, I even found that the gospel freed me from having to understand my freedom in order to possess it.

We are not justified by our understanding of God's grace, after all; we are justified by the death and resurrection of Christ!

SURELY YOU KNOW

After those painful months, I read the book of Job with new eyes and ears. Here was a man who had endured cataclysmic loss: financial loss, relational loss, emotional loss, physical loss—real devastation, tangible devastation. If we were to believe in comparative suffering (minimizing!), then Job wins. His life puts even our worst tragedies in perspective. Yes, even those of George Costanza. But he also puts our virtues in perspective. Job had lived a good life. He had done everything right. Even God declared Job righteous to the Devil's face. He was upright, successful, and a loving father. And then suddenly, he lost everything.

There is rarely a question of where God is when the sun is shining. When a couple marries, when a baby is born, or a better-paying job comes around—we always attribute these good things to God's sovereign work in our lives. And we are right to do so. But once life takes a turn for the worse—when a couple divorces, a child dies, we lose a job, or our health declines—suddenly we're not so sure if God really is sovereign, or good. Yet during Job's lengthy thirty-chapter lament, God seems to be sitting back silently and listening as Job and his friends battle back and forth, trying to figure out Why. If God really is there, why does He hide His face? Job cannot understand what is happening and demands an answer from God. If he can just understand what God is doing, he'll be okay. In the midst of the rocky transition at Coral Ridge, I, too, demanded an explanation from God. After all, I had done what He asked me to do—I had stepped out in faith. But what I didn't realize at the time is that explanations are ultimately a substitute for trust. All that I deeply longed for, what I really needed from God, I already had in Christ in what He accomplished on the cross two thousand years ago. But like many of you, I had forgotten that it still applied to me.

What God pressed deeply into me is that there is no true, lasting hope outside of Him. Specifically, there is no true, lasting hope outside of the death and resurrection of Jesus Christ. I'm not talking about an explanation of what happened on Calvary—I'm talking about Calvary itself. I had forgotten its scandal. Just think about it for a moment, Christian. The most vile, treasonous, darkest moment in the history of the world—the very event that appeared to be the most brutal defeat and failure—turned out to be the most gloriously life-giving event in all eternity. The salvation of the world taking place under the auspices of the most grotesque and tragic crime in human history. It is both breathtakingly beautiful and simple—our trespass for His righteousness, once and for all, with conversion consisting of that bittersweet realization that our sin was both the cause of the horror as well its merciful purpose. In other words, the cross is not something we can grasp until we are on our knees.

But imagine for a moment that God had given Job the explanation he desired. Let's say God had come to Job and said, *This is what you're going to experience; this is how it will happen to you; but just hold tight. It won't last forever, and in the end you will be sanctified; I will be glorified, and the Devil will be defeated. Just know that for thousands of years, My people will be talking about you, Job, so a little bit of pain is worth generations of pleasure.* What would Job have ultimately been putting his faith and trust in? What would have been helping him endure? Certainly not God alone. If Job had been given that explanation, he could have said to himself, *Well, if that's the good that's going to happen to me, if I'm going to get a double portion of everything I lost, then I'll endure, not for God's sake, but for my sake.*

This is the key to God's silence. God wanted Job to trust Him, come what might. He knew that it was the only way Job would ever survive his hours of darkness. Explanations, as we said earlier, are a substitute for trust, a red herring at best. God is interested in something much more powerful than anything information could ever produce. He is interested in faith. It should come as no surprise then, that when God finally broke His silence, it was to not to explain Himself. Quite the opposite, in fact:

> Then the LORD answered Job out of the storm.
> He said:
>
> "Who is this that darkens my counsel with words
> without knowledge?
> Brace yourself like a man; I will question you, and you
> shall answer me.
>
> "Where were you when I laid the earth's foundation?
> Tell me, if you understand.
> Who marked off its dimensions? Surely you know!"
> (Job 38:1–5a)

If you detect a whiff of divine sarcasm, you're not mistaken. God asked Job a series of questions that, at first glance, almost seem mean. But they were designed to show Job just how small and powerless he really was. God was not doing this for His own benefit. Job may have been on his knees, but his forehead wasn't to the ground yet. The Lord mercifully put to death Job's final idol—the idol of explanation. God liberated Job from the prison of Why. He liberated Job from himself. It was a glorious ruin.

Only when we come to the end of ourselves do we come to the beginning of God. This is a common theme in the Bible—desperation precedes deliverance. Grief precedes glory. The cross precedes the crown. Powerlessness is the beginning of freedom. This is not to say that every cloud has a silver lining, or some such nonsense. That would be a minimization. It is only to say that if the past five years have taught me anything, it is this: I would never have received any clarity about the beauty of the gospel if I hadn't first been forced to face the ugliness of my sin and idolatry at the foot of the cross. As the apostle Paul exclaimed in 1 Corinthians, "For the word of the cross is folly to those who are perishing, but to us who are being saved it is the power of God" (1:18 ESV).

So how about it? Ready to come and die with me yet? Be careful—you may get more than you bargained for.

NOTES

1. "Who Do You Think You Are?," *This American Life*, Chicago Public Radio, transcript, November 7, 2009, accessed June 5, 2012, http://www.thisamericanlife.org/radio-archives/episode/368/transcript.
2. "Who Do You Think You Are?," *This American Life*.
3. Ethan Richardson, *This American Gospel: Public Radio Parables and the Grace of God* (Charlottesville, VA: Mockingbird, 2012), 107.
4. Michael Horton, *A Place for Weakness* (Grand Rapids, MI: Zondervan, 2010), 37.

CHAPTER 7

THE GOSPEL OF SUFFERING

I've got a confession to make. The Coral Ridge transition was not my first experience with God using suffering to free me from myself. God has had to draw me, like an addict, back to the truth of who He is over and over again, often despite myself, and I have little doubt that He will continue to do so. Indeed, the "school of hard knocks" has convinced me that we never move beyond our need for Him and His intervention, and the beautiful reality of His inexhaustible grace.

At the beginning of the book, I mentioned getting the call from my father saying that, after forty-one years of marriage, he and my mother were separating. Separate they did, and soon after they got divorced. It was an incredibly painful, confusing, and emotionally draining time for me and my siblings. The separation was a total curveball. Our parents had provided a very happy, healthy, loving, stable home life during our upbringing. There had been no infidelity or abuse—in fact, we are still scratching our collective heads, wondering what exactly happened.

The months following my father's announcement were sad and awkward ones. My wife and I had just moved back to Fort Lauderdale to plant a church, which meant I was constantly running into people who knew my parents. They would ask about them, and I would avoid answering. If pressed, I would respond by saying they were having a tough time, that prayers would be appreciated. But when the final blow came and the divorce was made public, I started to dread that question with every fiber of my being. Each time I had to answer, I felt like I was grinding the words out. And every time I acknowledged the divorce out loud, it felt like I was losing a part of myself. It felt like death. Privately, I started questioning who I was, questioning everything I'd been taught, questioning the validity of my parents' faith. If their faith wasn't as robust as I thought it was, maybe the faith itself wasn't robust! I was living inside *The Sixth Sense*, reinterpreting all that had come before through this unexpected twist.

I remember going to see Larry Crabb, who was in a practice with my father. "How's your mom and dad doing?" Larry asked.

"Larry, I don't know what to do. Seriously. I feel like my whole world has been turned upside down. I don't get this. It's excruciating."

Larry said something remarkable. He could see that I was trapped in the prison of Why, banging my head against the bars. He said, "Tullian, listen to me: the 'why' is none of your concern. This is not your burden to fix or figure out. You are not responsible for your parents' relationship or their reputation, or even your own reputation. Those are in God's hands, and His ways are His, not ours. When it comes to God's will, the sooner you can get out of the conjecture business, the better. *If you don't go to your grave confused, you don't go to your grave trusting.* Painful as it is, this situation gives you an opportunity to show them grace, to love them in their brokenness in a new way. Which is precisely what Jesus has done for you and continues to do for you." Larry preached the gospel to me that day, and it made all the difference.

With Larry's permission—that is, with the assurance that God was not waiting for me to solve our family problems—I came to realize that my struggles went beyond my sadness over the dissolution of my parents' four decades of marriage. Much of what was so devastating was the blow to my personal identity, which was intricately wrapped up in being their son. My folks had enjoyed good standing in society; they were devout churchgoing people, of national repute. I grew up seeing my mother on *Good Morning America*, so classy, so beautiful, so talented. Then there was my father: European, sophisticated, PhD, the most intuitive person I knew. As far as I was concerned, they hung the moon. Being their son gave me a sense of significance and security. More than that, though, I had made it into an idol.

What? How do you make an idol out of your parents? Idolatry, after all, conjures up all sorts of antiquated images of golden calves and prehistoric rituals. Yet while it may be an anachronistic word, it is far from an anachronistic problem. Tim

Keller has written insightfully about contemporary idolatry: "Sin isn't only doing bad things, it is more fundamentally making good things into ultimate things. Sin is building your life and meaning on anything, even a very good thing, more than on God."[1] I had enjoyed being a part of my family, which is fine and good. But the suffering I endured during their divorce revealed that it had become too important to me. While I may not have necessarily idolized my parents, I certainly idolized what they provided for me. I worshipped the good reputation I had by virtue of being their child.

The Lord graciously dismantled this idol. And I thought I was free and clear for a time, and maybe I was. But like a game of cosmic Whac-A-Mole, my heart soon gravitated toward new idols, which would be exposed and demolished during the Coral Ridge transition. And clearly He's not done with me yet! It took these defeats for me to realize that the purpose of the Christian life is not to move beyond our need for God's grace and forgiveness. No, we move deeper into our dependency. This is the radical goodness of a God who is not interested in a better you, but a new you.

GOD MAKES US CRY UNCLE SO THAT WE MIGHT CRY ABBA

My friend Scotty Smith has said that *God will use pain in our lives to make us cry uncle so that we might cry Father.* At first, this may not seem like good news at all. Why would God allow pain into our lives to drive us to Him? It seems so backward! But Christians serve an unrelenting God who graciously disallows full, lasting satisfaction in anything but Him. And He often brings this about through affliction—our hearts being so hard and stubborn that nothing else will do the trick, to paraphrase Flannery O'Connor. Or as Steve Brown said, in his book *A Scandalous Freedom*:

> Pain is not something most people like. That is why we run from it as fast as we can. That is also why we aren't free. Jesus hardly ever goes to those places where we run.
>
> When pain comes (or when we fear that it will come), don't run away. Run to it, and you will find you have run into the arms of Jesus.... Then you will laugh and dance in the freedom and the reality of God's sufficiency and the power that becomes awesome in your weakness.[2]

It's a paradox. Our point of pain reveals to us our greatest need—our need to be set free from false hopes and to cling to the only hope of the gospel. But we often settle for the counterfeit of nonpain. Think for a moment about your last day on earth. What kind of life do you hope to have lived? Mine would look something like this:

- I want to be happy and fulfilled in a relationship with my spouse. To love and be loved in return.

- I hope to have a good relationship with my children, keep them safe, and live long enough to see that they turn out okay.
- I hope to have accomplished something meaningful and important with my work. I would like to leave the world a slightly better place than I found it.
- I hope never to be poor. It would be nice to leave something for those who come after.
- I hope that I die in my sleep so that I don't experience any pain.

Naturally, we all want comfort, achievement, and as little stress as possible. And that's not necessarily a bad thing. But isn't it odd that the presence of Jesus doesn't even register? Sure, some of us may feel obligated to pay Jesus lip service. "It goes without saying!" But the unspoken hope is that Jesus will deliver on our felt needs of comfort, that He will serve as the dispenser of rewards rather than the reward itself. C. S. Lewis was on to something when he claimed that our desires aren't too great; they're too weak: "If we consider the unblushing promises of reward and the staggering nature of the rewards promised in the Gospels, it would seem that Our Lord finds our desires not too strong, but too weak. We are half-hearted creatures, fooling about with drink and sex and ambition when infinite joy is offered us, like an ignorant child who wants to go on making mud pies in a slum because he cannot imagine what is meant by the offer of a holiday at the sea. We are far too easily pleased."[3]

God is more concerned with our knowing Him than He is in our half-hearted pleasures of comfort, ambition, and success. So much so that He often allows pain and suffering into our lives to clear the clutter of mute, deaf, and unworthy idols that can never deliver on their promises, even when they're ostensibly good things like health, family, career, success, and status.

Job knew that he was not entitled to anything he had—God held the title to everything. His money, his relationships, his place in society, his family were all on loan from God. And as an owner of nothing and a steward of everything, he was able to say with sincerity, "I came with nothing from the womb, / I go with nothing to the tomb. / God gave me children freely, then / He took them to himself again. At last I taste the bitter rod, / My wise and ever blessed God."[4] While he loved his health and children and reputation and role and wealth, he didn't locate his identity in those things.

If the foundation of our identity is anything less than God—if the thing that makes us who we are is a position in life, a certain relationship, a prestigious (if difficult to pronounce!) last name, money, you name it—then we will experience pain whenever and wherever that foundation is assaulted, as it inevitably will be. Our suffering will serve as an indication of how little we actually believe this good news, or at least an indicator of what we are building our life on and where we are looking for meaning. And when we lose something that we believed was crucial to our existence and value, maybe even something that we felt we deserved, when one of the load-bearing beams in the house that glory built collapses, we will become embittered or despondent. The truth is, suffering does not rob us of joy; idolatry does.

But if our identity is anchored in Christ, so that we are able to say, "Everything I need I already possess in Him," then suffering will drive us deeper into our source of joy. When theologians talk about God "imputing" His righteousness to us through the death and resurrection of Christ, this is what they mean: that our identity, and therefore our freedom, is not a matter of Why or How but Who. Our ultimate standing has been secured—from the outside—and nothing we may do or say can shake the foundations that were built two thousand years ago. We are freed to revel in our expendability! Indeed, the gospel alone provides us with the foundation to maintain radical joy in remarkable loss. The late, great theologian Gerhard Forde wrote masterfully about this counterintuitive aspect of God's work:

> The foolishness of God in the cross is wiser than the wisdom of the world. The righteousness that avails before God is a being claimed by the crucified and resurrected Christ. It is not like accomplishing something but like dying and coming to life. It is not like earning something but more like falling in love. It is not the attainment of a long-sought goal, the arrival at the end of a process, but the beginning of something

> absolutely new, something never before heard of or entertained....
>
> Grace says, "believe it" and everything—EVERYTHING!—is already done. It is the creative Word of God. If that doesn't work then nothing will.... The theologian of the cross knows that the love of God creates precisely out of nothing. Therefore the sinner must be reduced to nothing in order to be saved.... [This] is the hope of the resurrection. God brings life out of death. He calls into being that which is from that which is not. In order that there be a resurrection, the sinner must die. All presumption must be ended. The truth must be seen.[5]

The death Forde talks about certainly has to do with our bodies, with physical death and decay, but it also has to do with our aspirations and hopes and idols. These things must be put to death before we can be resurrected to new life. God demolishes the old, so that He might give new life. The theology of the cross announces that "disaster becomes the pre-condition for a new, unfettered life."[6] In addiction language, bottoming out always precedes sobriety.

Unfortunately, like a bottoming-out experience, the theology of the cross cannot be prescribed, only described. God does not work according to our timetable or perception of events. We cannot "game the system," as much as we might like to. No one wants his parents to get divorced. No one chooses to be thrown out of her church. The hiddenness of God resists our attempts to see through it; it must be endured. Jesus really did suffer and die. He was not checking His watch.

THE TRAGIC REDUCTION OF THE GOSPEL

Something has gone wrong in our understanding of this gloriously backward economy. We have gotten it into our heads that after we face the dark side of sin at conversion, everything turns up roses from then on. We view conversion as the starting point of an upward-sloping journey in which Christians experience victory over sin, perfect health, meaningful marriages, and successful businesses (or church mergers!). We have absorbed the karmic notion that the Christian life is a steadily ascending staircase to actions and consequences, self-fulfillment and human progress.

Again, I was not (and am not) immune to these toxic assumptions. It took the repeated defeats of my adult life for me to even begin to grasp the sustaining power of the good news, that God's grace doesn't expire after the first conversion or nervous breakdown. This is such good news! You see, along with the vast majority of professing Christians, I had reduced the gospel to what non-Christians must believe in order to be saved before moving into the deeper waters of sanctification. But suffering taught me that the only deeper waters are those of our own need: none of us ever grow to a place where we no longer require the 200-proof version of God's mercy and forgiveness. The gospel is not a message reserved for those Sundays when you're encouraged to bring your unbelieving friend. It is the *only* message! For both the non-Christian *and* the Christian. As our idols reveal to us, we all have some corner of our lives where we need to be converted afresh, where some false hope needs to die if faith is to be born. This side of the pearly gates, you and I can be relied upon to forget the goodness of the gospel. Like factories, our hearts, to paraphrase John Calvin, will never cease to produce new idols. Our only hope lies in hearing the crushing word of the Law and the absolving word of the gospel every day. Every minute!

As an aside, this is precisely why churches need to preach the basic gospel every Sunday. Sermons with advice (or "application") about relationships or money or social justice will always fall flat, regardless of how sound the advice may be. They do not take into account the depth of suffering experienced in the life of a believer or the sin that persists in every Christian. Martin Luther spoke of this reality as our being simultaneously saint and sinner, justified and sinful. Paul Zahl translated Luther's meaning into modern language when he said we are all Christians and human beings at the same time.[7] This means that the Old Adam is always on the prowl, scrounging for some new law by which to justify himself apart from Christ. And he dies hard! If the assumption from the pulpit is that conversion is a onetime-only event, the messages will revolve around what the Christian needs to do ("Ten Steps to a Happier Marriage" or "Five Ways to Promote Peace" or even "Six Tenants of Second Temple Judaism"), rather than what Christ has done. Esteemed author Marilynne Robinson expressed this sad predicament via the following insight: "I have a theory that the churches fill on Christmas and Easter because it is on these days that the two most startling moments in the Christian narrative can be heard again."[8]

In other words, people come to church on major holidays not solely out of a sense of social and religious propriety, but because, at least subconsciously, those are the two days when they can be assured of hearing some good news from the pulpit, as opposed to a spiritualized version of the instruction coming from every other voice in the culture, including the ones inside of us. All this to say, if you attend a church where you're not hearing the gospel regularly, it might be time to find a new place to worship. Because when the "big hurt" comes, you're going to need it!

BEAUTY AMID UGLINESS: THE CROSS-CENTERED LIFE OF JESUS

Perhaps it sounds like I'm going overboard. What about the rest of Jesus's life? He did more than just die! He performed miracles and healed people. There were certainly some glorious moments of nonsuffering scattered throughout the accounts of His life and ministry. Fair enough. In fact, praise God that there were!

But let's take a step back and reflect for a moment. If you were the Son of God, how would you have entered the world? What would you have accomplished? Who would you have influenced, and what would other people have thought of you? Odds are, we would have made sure we were born to highly influential, brilliant parents whose faces would have graced the covers of *Time* magazine for their great feats of humanitarian aid. If not somewhere glamorous, then we would have at least been born someplace dignified. And if we really wanted to do the most good, we would have been sure to attend the best schools, receive the highest academic honors, and generally put ourselves in a position to garner the most possible support for our cause. Maybe while attending said prestigious school, we might invent a website that billions and billions of people would join, where we could influence our friends and followers with the click of a button. Wait a second … that's *our* version of the entrance of the savior into the world. One thing's for certain: this version wouldn't include any pain.

But how did *Jesus* arrive? He was born to a teenaged virgin girl in a glorified garage and laid in a feeding trough. Jesus grew up in a rural area, never held a public office or wrote a book. He was broke and virtually homeless. All the religious leaders hated Him, and when He got embroiled in religious and political controversy, His best and only friends abandoned Him. Which is when He was arrested and brought up on false charges before being unjustly executed as a common criminal. *Lackluster* would be a nice word for Christ's origins. One can't help but wonder if the disciples felt disappointed. I certainly would have been. Jesus was supposed to be the Messiah, after all. I would have urged Him to raise a guerrilla army and set up a new kingdom of justice and peace by force. We'd roll into Jerusalem in style; there would be no mistaking our entrance. But instead, Jesus told the disciples that if you want to be great, you have to be humble.

He didn't ride into town on a strong, beautiful white horse and an entourage of beautiful people. He was carried by a donkey. Lackluster! Fortunately, I wasn't given a say in the plan.

Our dreams are a window into our theology. We are a proud people, the inheritors of the American Dream—the pursuit of happiness is our inalienable right. Like bratty, self-involved little kids, we push past the Giver to grab for the gift. Can you see it? We use God for health, wealth, and emotional well-being, and in the process, we miss out on relationship with our heavenly Father. This optimistic, get-'er-done, blessings-addicted faith has had many faces throughout history. In 1518, Martin Luther described our default theology as one bent on self-glory that serves as a framework for *our* personal blessing, catering to a false idea of control and casting God as a servant to our desire. This stands in stark contrast to the theology of the cross, where according to 1 Corinthians 1, God's wisdom is foolish, and He sends the great hope of the world—the only hope!—a dying savior.

> But God chose what is foolish in the world to shame the wise; God chose what is weak in the world to shame the strong; God chose what is low and despised in the world, even things that are not, to bring to nothing things that are, so that no human being might boast in the presence of God. (1 Cor. 1:27–29 ESV)

God saw fit to enter into suffering through Christ and out of that suffering birth something beautiful.

The Corinthians were not unlike you and me. Like us, they were addicted to themselves. Like us, they deferred to their skills, talents, abilities, and the results they can produce. Just like us, they were convinced that God shows up in flashy ways, that He's impressed with how cultured we are, how beautiful our churches look, and how eloquent our speakers sound. Don't believe me? Again, think about the personal testimonies in your church. When was the last time someone gave the microphone to the poor guy with chronic health issues? Or the recently bankrupt businessman? Like the Corinthians, our religion is the way of the glory road. We love success stories; we love a good comeback. But for the most part, the God of the repeat offender keeps silent in our churches. How strange, then, that the apostle Paul resigned himself to know nothing but Christ and Him crucified! He genuinely seemed to believe that God shows up in the most counterintuitive of ways: in the defeat and weakness of the cross.[9]

Fortunately for the downtrodden and addicted, Paul was not whistling "Dixie." God does not get things done in the world by merely adding a new coat of paint; He brings the house down to the foundation so He can build something new. God does not argue with us so that we take our medicine and get well. He raises us from the dead! God doesn't give us advice about how to overcome; in the gospel, Jesus has already overcome! Amid our glorious ruin, Jesus is strong, so we're free to be weak; Jesus won, so we're free to lose; Jesus was a somebody, so we can be a nobody; Jesus was extraordinary, so we are free to be ordinary; and Jesus succeeded for us, so we are free to fail!

Rather than run from the inevitability of life's tragedies, we are invited to face them, head-on, with hope. We can even begin to call things what they are—rather than what we *wish* them to be. A theology of the cross might seem brutal and ugly to those coasting through life. But to the compulsive, hurting, sin-sick sufferer, the cross is a beacon of hope and rest like no other. Scratch that—*the man hanging on the cross* is a beacon of hope and rest like no other.

NOTES

1. Tim Keller, "Talking about Idolatry in a Postmodern Age," Monergism, April 2001, accessed June 5, 2012, http://www.monergism.com/postmodernidols.html.
2. Steve Brown, *A Scandalous Freedom* (West Monroe, LA: Howard Books, 2004), 216.
3. C. S. Lewis, "The Weight of Glory," in *The Weight of Glory, and Other Addresses* (Grand Rapids, MI: Eerdmans, 1965), 1–2.
4. John Piper, "Job, Part 1," *Desiring God*, November 27, 1994, accessed June 6, 2012, http://www.desiringgod.org/resource-library/poems/job-part-1.
5. Gerhard O. Forde, *On Being a Theologian of the Cross: Reflections on Luther's Heidelberg Disputation, 1518* (Grand Rapids, MI: Eerdmans, 1997), 105–15.

6. "Now Available! The Merciful Impasse: The Sermon on the Mount for People Who've Crashed (and Burned)," *Mockingbird*, November 4, 2011, accessed June 6, 2012, http://www.mbird.com/2011/11/now-available-the-merciful-impasse-the-sermon-on-the-mount-for-people-whove-crashed-and-burned/.
7. Paul Zahl, "Love Your Enemies, Part 1," in *The Merciful Impasse: The Sermon on the Mount for Those Who've Crashed (and Burned)* (Charlottesville, VA: Mockingbird, 2011), CD-ROM.
8. Marilynne Robinson, *When I Was a Child I Read Books* (New York: Farrar, Straus and Giroux, 2012). 126–27.
9. Justin S. Holcomb and Lindsey A. Holcomb, *Rid of My Disgrace* (Wheaton, IL: Crossway, 2011), 57. Justin and Lindsey Holcomb wrote: "The Bible teaches that our suffering is a place to experience God's sustaining grace in our weakness. It is clearly taught that grief is a natural response when one experiences loss, but it can be tempered by the knowledge of Christ and the resurrection" (p. 60).

CHAPTER 8

WEIGHTY MERCIES

On the night of July 23, 1986, the American short-story writer Andre Dubus was driving from Boston to his home in Haverhill, Massachusetts, when he stopped to assist an injured couple on the side of the road.

As he was carrying the first passenger to safety, an oncoming car swerved and hit them. Dubus was able to push his charge out of harm's way in time, but her copassenger, still in the car, was killed instantly. The collision crushed both of Dubus's legs, putting him in a wheelchair, where he would battle both chronic infection and clinical depression for the rest of his life. Exhausted by the emotional and physical toll of it all, his third wife would leave him, taking with her their two young daughters.

During this time, Dubus also underwent a conversion to Christianity, or at least a marked deepening of his faith. In an essay written after the accident he testified:

> Living in the world as a cripple allows you to see more clearly the crippled hearts of some people

> whose bodies are whole and sound. All of us, from time to time, suffer this crippling. Some suffer it daily and nightly; and while most of us, nearly all of us, have compassion and love in our hearts, we cannot or will not see these barely visible wounds of other human beings, and so cannot or will not pick up the telephone or travel to someone's home or write a note or make some other seemingly trifling gesture to give someone what only we, and God, can give: an hour's respite, or a day's, or a night's; and sometimes more than respite: sometimes joy.[1]

It is no stretch to say that Andre Dubus understood a thing or two about the theology of the cross. Not necessarily because he grasped it intellectually, but because he had lived it. Suffering accomplished in him what nothing else could, a softening of his heart, a newfound compassion for fellow sufferers.

Brokenness precedes usefulness. It just does. Who reaches out to parents who have lost children to drunken driving accidents? Other parents who have lost children to drunken-driving accidents. When we go through something painful and when God breaks us, it makes us both more useful to others and more willing to be used. We are able to empathize and sympathize and lend insight and help and perspective to other people. Take a poll of people you know in ministry, and I guarantee you'll find that some kind of painful experience informed their sense of call. People minister out of their own suffering, not despite it.

I hope we have established by this point that God works through disaster and defeat, that He is in the death and resurrection business. In this chapter, we'll take a look at how precisely He does so: the fruit of this gospel of suffering or, you might say, a few of the ways that the cross transforms suffering. Of course, there is a danger here in succumbing to the very thing we've have been decrying, namely, turning suffering into the first step on the road to improved circumstances or character, or assigning some hindsight, silver-lining-like Why to painful events. But again, we are not talking about freedom from suffering; we are talking about freedom in and through suffering. And when suffering is turned into a means to an end—or even an elaborate illustration of a theological standpoint—there is no real surrender or death. God is not mocked; the theology of the cross cannot be manipulated. Dubus never got out of his wheelchair.

SUFFERING LIBERATES US FROM TRIVIALITY

Suffering not only has a way of liberating us from the things that enslave us, but also has a way of liberating us from the petty concerns and worries that bog down our everyday existence. What's important often rises to the top. I got a glimpse of this when I watched my friend Jenny deal with a brain tumor. I vividly remember a conversation with her where she recalled the period of depression she had experienced just prior to her diagnosis. The bad news arrived, and suddenly she received crystal clarity about her life. It's not that she no longer battled depression, hopelessness, and difficulty. Far from it! She suffered multiple operations and brutal rounds of incapacitating treatments. But the conversations we had in her last months were some of the most focused, authentic of my life. The tumor had unburdened her of her fears. She had been given more perspective; she wasn't "sweating the small stuff." She spoke to me from the heart, with no artifice or pretension. I've heard the same thing from a number of her friends since she died. They visited Jenny under the assumption that she needed their encouragement. But they were the ones who walked away from their visits encouraged!

If you're detecting any of the flippant triumphalism that we so often hear when such stories are reported on television—you know, someone with a terminal illness who just won't be slowed down and always stays positive—please forgive me. We love those stories because we can't bear to look at the realities of sickness and death; we just have to put a "triumph of the human spirit" spin on things. This wasn't the case with Jenny. She was sick, she knew it, and she spoke of her impending death with a stark, realistic tone. But she was able to say with complete sincerity that God had used her illness to wake her up. We talked about that a lot. The sickness itself was an enemy that ravaged her body. She would be leaving behind her husband and extended family, but God had not abandoned her. He had cleared away all the idolatrous clutter in her life. Her career ambition, her reputation, her prideful short fuse. What God did in her life during that time was a miracle. We often hear about how poverty for some great souls is a blessing. For most, it's what it is, a curse. And every now and then, terminal illness like Jenny's ennobles its victim. But Jenny didn't get to that place through happy-clappy sentimentality; her journey took her straight through the valley of the shadow of death. In fact, early on, her cries sounded more like those of an atheist than someone of faith. But thank God her cries were free of pious Christian sentimentality.

At the end of her life, God gave Jenny a deeper, more abiding love for Him and other people. It was so strange, sitting there, listening to the priest during her memorial service. On one hand, I knew that Jenny's tumor was a real enemy, a tragic reality of living in a fallen world. And yet that illness had woken Jenny up to God, to her own life, and to others.

Pain and suffering loosen our grip on this temporal life. Deeper suffering can lead to deeper surrender. In time, our career aspirations and our personal opinions become less important. Our bodies age, our joints stiffen and ache, our eyes grow dim, digestion slows, and sleep becomes difficult. Yet at the same time, the ups and downs of daily life grow smaller and smaller. With each new pain and health complication, the world becomes less inviting as the next life becomes more appealing. In its own way, pain paves the way for a graceful departure (Eccles. 12:1–14). Death, after all, is not the end but the threshold of a new day.

GOD'S "DREADFUL WITHDRAWAL" AND THE GIFT OF GRIEF

Take the book of Job. Some commentators actually become exasperated with Job because it seems to go on and on and on, endlessly repeating the same arguments without providing any definitive answers. There's just chapter after chapter of Job and his friends covering the same territory over and over again. But the redundancy serves both a theological and a literary purpose. Yes, it does goes on, and on and on, with no definitive answers—which is exactly how many of us experience suffering in real life. That is, you are in good company. Job wasn't given a definitive answer either. God did not come to him at the end of the book and say, *You made it, Job! Now let Me tell you the real reason why you suffered.* All we find at the bottom of Job's suffering is a naked longing for God. Which, it turns out, is enough.

Job's cry is not, "God, why have You ruined my life?" His cry is, "God, why have You left me?" He doesn't miss his livelihood and possessions so much as the thick presence of God. Notice that Job never questions whether or not God is in control. In fact, the very fact that he knows God is in absolute control is what causes him so much pain. So even in his lament, he's demonstrating confidence in God. Notice what he said in chapter 29, verses 2 through 6.

> Oh, that I were as in the months of old,
>   as in the days when God watched over me,
> when his lamp shown upon my head,
>   and by his light I walk through darkness,
> as I was in my prime,
>   when the friendship of God was upon my tent,
> when the Almighty was yet with me,
>   when my children were all around me,

> when my steps were washed with butter,
> and the rock poured out for me streams of oil! (ESV)

In light of everything that Job had lost, what he felt most acutely was God's absence. He was expressing the same kind of depression that overtook the psalmist in Psalm 88. In verses 13 and 14 it says, "But I, O LORD, cry to you; in the morning my prayer comes before you. O LORD, why do you cast my soul away? Why do you hide your face from me?" (ESV). Did you know that it's okay to pray that way when you feel it? The psalmist did and so did Job. The Bible sanctions desperate prayers—prayers in what the Puritans used to call "God's dreadful withdrawal." And all of us have experienced those seasons of life when God seems to be silent. Yet if there is a longing for God to come back, it means that we know Him, because if we did not know God, there would be no longing for His return. We would not have known what nearness to God was in the first place; the distance wouldn't bother us. In His absence, our appreciation, dependence, and affection for God are increased, which leads to greater freedom and liberation.

When God pulls away from His children—in those seasons of His dreadful withdrawal—we often find ourselves crying for His return with great intensity, maybe even desperation. Again, this is the key difference between a lament and a complaint. Lamenting is a cry *for* God; complaining is a cry *against* God. In his lament, Job would rather not live at all than live in a world without the thick, comforting presence of God in the most difficult times.

In other words, God withdraws from us in order to make our souls long for Him even more. But this is not some cosmic game of cat and mouse, some theologized version of "playing it cool." Heaven forbid! No, instead of relieving us from our problems, God intends to demonstrate His sufficiency in our problems.

No one understood this more profoundly than William Cowper, the eighteenth-century hymnist and poet, who wrote many, many hymns and was a dear friend of John "Amazing Grace" Newton. Cowper suffered terribly with depression his entire life. He tried killing himself on three different occasions. And after one of his failed suicides attempts, he wrote what has become one of my favorite hymns: "God Moves in a Mysterious Way." Listen to where he finds his rest in the midst of hopelessness.

God moves in a mysterious way
His wonders to perform;
He plants His footsteps in the sea
And rides upon the storm.
Deep in unfathomable mines
Of never failing skill
He treasures up His bright designs
And works His sovereign will.
Ye fearful saints, fresh courage take;
The clouds ye so much dread
Are big with mercy and shall break
In blessings on your head.
Judge not the Lord by feeble sense,

But trust Him for His grace;
Behind a frowning providence,
He hides a smiling face.[2]

You may be at a place in your life where the promises of the Bible seem completely foreign or at least shrouded in mystery. Your sense of God is feeble at best. You can't relate to Job. You no longer care about the theology that might be contained in your present suffering; you no longer care about suffering "correctly" or nonselfishly; you simply want the pain to end! If you are that person, you are not alone. There is hope! And it doesn't require your understanding anything. It doesn't require anything of you, in fact, because it required everything of Jesus.

Jesus experienced God's withdrawal in a way that none of us can possibly fathom. Before climbing Golgotha, He had experienced nothing but the Father's unrelenting love. But on the cross, Jesus cried out in agony as the sin of the world was placed upon Him, "My God, my God, why have you forsaken me" (Matt. 27:46).

Jesus suffered the full brunt of the Father's unrelenting wrath for sinners like you and me; He experienced a withdrawal far more serious and dreadful than any you or I or even Job ever experienced. And He suffered this withdrawal on our behalf, so that you and I would never have to experience God's terminal silence. Where once there was punishment and annihilation, now rings that glorious refrain: I will never leave you; I will never forsake you (Heb. 13:5).

GRIEF AND WORSHIP

There is a short, powerful phrase that comes just after the hammer falls on Job that sums up this liberating conception of grief. Job's children are gone. His wealth and property, all gone. Shirt torn. "He fell to the ground in worship" (Job 1:20).

Say what?

There is an assumption out there that worship can take place only when you've got a smile on your face. If that were true, two-thirds of the Psalms would be heretical.[3] Instead, the Psalms are filled to the brim with words that lament failure, pain, betrayal, and human brokenness. The Bible teaches us that grief and worship are not opposed, that they actually go hand in hand. Grief can be heard as a cry for what once was, and one day will be again, a world without pain and disease and conflict, a world characterized by shalom. Grief acknowledges the catastrophic state of affairs east of Eden. God does not expect us to keep a stiff upper lip in times of trouble; He is not pleased with robotic attempts to exonerate Him in the midst of pain. We cry uncle so that we might cry Abba!

In the moment of tragedy, most of us actually respond fairly calmly. But check back with us a week or two later, after the relatives have left town and the neighbors have stopped bringing meals. That's when we unravel. It can take us a long time to process painful events, and that's okay. I watched this with my wife, Kim, when her father died eleven years ago. For the first ten or twelve days after her dad died, she was so strong for the rest of her family. After that, she just fell apart. God graciously allowed for the shock she experienced to serve her so she was able to make it through the trying times and be strong for others. But then it came time for her to really deal with the grief, and she was undone.

My father was a psychologist, and he used to say that character is demonstrated more by our reactions than our actions. He understood that who we really are comes out in times of pain and desperation. Or as Alan Redpath, a pastor up in Chicago many years ago, used to say, "The flavor of a teabag comes out best when put in hot water." Job's worshipful response to his tribulation is absolutely stunning. If his response didn't include grief over his loss, we might conclude that his "worship" was simply an expression of shock—that the magnitude of the situation hadn't really hit him yet. Instead, God carefully, generously, and graciously inspired the text to include Job's emotional outburst before his expression of worship, which gives it its authenticity. No, the grief Job experienced was real, which is precisely why it gave birth to such a theologically deep, worshipful response. There is almost something joyful about that phrase—*he worshipped.*

I have a hard time relating. I hear Job's response as law ("ought"), and therefore accusation. Do you? For me, his exemplary reaction begs the question: What allowed him to absorb such pain while maintaining a worshipful stance? Was he simply a fundamentally better person than you and I? How is it that amid the rubble of a ruined life some believers honestly experience a sense of joy? Once again, the answer lies in the Who, not the How.

It turns out that Job's gravitation toward the Who is not so much a matter of virtue as it might seem. Once he finally gives up on receiving any explanation from God, his laments turn into cries for vindication from the moralistic assumptions and accusations of his friends. His friends have made their feelings known: "Job, fix yourself up, you clean up your act, get it straight, and God will return to you and give you back a life of blessing." But Job, the good theologian that he is, recognizes that there is nothing he can do to make himself right before God. God is holy and perfect while human beings are imperfect and sinful. He says, "If one wished to contend with him, one could not answer him once in a thousand times" (9:3 ESV). In other words, even if he had a good argument, Job knew that he could not contend with God, because of his limitations as a sinner. And if his friends think that he can or should resort to performance to gain back God's favor, then they do not know God. It was not Job's good behavior that earned God's favor in the first place.

While at first glance it might seem as though Job was throwing in the towel, these verses are utterly gospel saturated. They remind us that there is nothing we can do that can make God love us, to earn His favor, or to gain His approval. Which is precisely why Job, in his darkest hour, appealed to the future rescuer, arbiter, and advocate God promised in Genesis 3:15. Job didn't know who this redeemer was supposed to be; all he saw was a vague black-and-white figure appearing on the horizon. He wasn't clinging to some pie-in-the-sky idea of redemption; rather, he clung to the promise that there is something (Someone) looming larger than the tragedy. We readers are privileged to look back and know that he was seeing Jesus Christ. *He* is the redeemer who will right all the wrongs, dry every tear, and bring vindication for those who have been afflicted by the inexplicable pain and disaster.

When Jesus rose from death, He was the first human being to be fully vindicated as the Son of God. But the story doesn't end there. Romans 8:29 says that He is the "firstborn among many brothers," which means, as His people, we are adopted into God's family with Jesus, our faithful brother, representing us to the Father. Christ is our mediator, He is our arbiter, He is our heavenly defense attorney. He has done for sinners what we could never do for ourselves. Even if you were to clean up your act and do everything straight, perform well, obey, get better, or suffer well (whatever that means), none of that effort will work. Because in the end, we are all sinners in need of rescue, and of ultimate vindication. Suffering has a way of stripping all resources away from us so that in the end, all that we have is the only thing that matters: the approval of God based on the accomplished work of Jesus. Our sin, our imperfection, isn't counted against us! My hope and prayer for you is that even amid your suffering, you would be gripped by the glorious news of the gospel, that before God you are clothed with perfection, and when God sees you, He sees the righteousness of His only Son.

ANTICIPATION OF FUTURE REDEMPTION

The note of worship heard in our grief is the same note of longing heard in times of God's dreadful withdrawal. It is a cry for Jesus to return. In Romans 8, Paul told us that all of creation is groaning in anticipation of its future redemption.[4] He even ends his first letter to the Corinthians with the plea "Maranatha! Lord Jesus, come quickly!" (see 1 Cor. 16:22). Paul was not exercising cold stoicism in this passage. There is nothing shameful about his expression of grief. No, he was *presupposing* brokenness, pain, and suffering. He was acknowledging that pain, suffering, and the brokenness of the world are very real. Yet we read in the same chapter that the coming kingdom will be so glorious that our present suffering will pale in comparison. "Always pain before a child is born" is how Bono puts it in the U2 song "Yahweh."[5] Revelation 21 describes the redemption of the world in stunning terms:

> Then I saw a new heaven and a new earth, for the first heaven and the first earth had passed away, and the sea was no more. And I saw the holy city, new Jerusalem, coming down out of heaven from God, prepared as a bride adorned for her husband. And I heard a loud voice from the throne saying, "Behold, the dwelling place of God is with man. He will dwell with them, and they will be his people, and God himself will be with them as their God. He will wipe away every

> tear from their eyes, and death shall be no more, neither shall there be mourning, nor crying, nor pain anymore, for the former things have passed away. (1–4 ESV)

The evangelist linked the reality of grief with the reality of anticipation. He viewed our tears as a sign of our aching for that place where children don't die of preventable diseases, where there is no more loss, theft, or violence. In a roundabout way, our cries of grief are statements of faith that God in Christ is making all things new, that one day all that causes us pain and discomfort will be put away forever. We've spoken about the danger of Romans 8:28; now it's time for the beauty. "And we know that for those who love God all things work together for good, for those who are called according to his purpose" (ESV). And that, Christian, is all you need to know.

To say that all things work together for our good may seem simplistic, and the temptation to use the verse in that way is incredibly strong, as we have discussed already. But there's a difference between simplicity and being simplistic. It's simple—it's not easy. In fact, earlier in the chapter, Paul described life as hard and full of suffering, with the creation itself groaning as it waits for redemption! Yet in comparison with our future glory, he told us, our troubles are only a blip on the radar. As Mother Teresa once said, "In light of heaven, the worst suffering on earth, a life full of the most atrocious tortures on earth, will be seen to be no more serious than one night in an inconvenient hotel."[6]

This is where the rubber meets the road. We can talk about death and resurrection until we are blue in the face, but we cannot ignore the reality that life sometimes feels like one long death, *sans* resurrection. Instead of finding ourselves filled with compassion for others, we find ourselves filled with jealousy and anger. The defeats we suffer leave us bloodied and bruised and self-protective rather than self-forgetful. In sickness we withdraw and become more bitter and fearful, rather than wise and surrendering. We shudder at God's absence until that's all we know. No amount of grace seems to make the pain go away.

Listen to me, dear friend. Our hope does not lie in this temporal life; it lies in the life to come. And sometimes that is all the consolation there is. Suffering takes us to the edge of eternity and confronts us with the horror of a life filled with arbitrary pain. But if the end of this life brings us to the threshold of eternity, then the most fortunate people in the universe are those who discover, through suffering, that this life is not all we have to live for. Those who find themselves and their eternal God through suffering have not suffered meaninglessly. Their poverty, grief, despair, and hunger have driven them to the Lord of eternity. Consider these words from Peter Kreeft.

> Now suppose both death and hell were utterly defeated. Suppose the fight was fixed. Suppose God took you on a crystal ball trip into your future and you saw with indubitable certainty that despite everything—your sin, your

> smallness, your stupidity—you could have free for the asking your whole crazy heart's deepest desire: heaven, eternal joy. Would you not return fearless and singing? What can earth do to you if you are guaranteed heaven? To fear the worst earthly loss would be like a millionaire fearing the loss of a penny—less, a scratch on a penny.[7]

Perhaps the only solace you can draw from suffering is that you begin to see that we were truly made for another world. You are right not to be satisfied until you are feasting with the rest of the saints, with King Jesus residing at the head of the table.

This, dear Christian, is what you were made for.

And all the ruin in the world cannot compare to the glory of that great day.

NOTES

1. Andre Dubus, "A Woman in April" in *Broken Vessels* (Boston: David R. Gondine, 1992), 143.
2. William Cowper, "God Moves in a Mysterious Way," *Cyber Hymnal*, accessed June 6, 2012, http://www.cyberhymnal.org/htm/g/m/gmovesmw.htm.
3. Justin and Lindsey Holcomb wrote: "Many of the psalms reveal the compassionate disposition of God toward those who suffer: 'The LORD is near to the brokenhearted and saves the crushed in spirit.' [Ps. 34:18.] Suffering does not repel God. Instead it draws God near. God promises never

to cut himself off from those who cry to him in distress" (*Rid of My Disgrace* [Wheaton, IL: Crossway, 2011], 57).

4. Justin and Lindsey Holcomb wrote: "If your future is based on Christ, you can have hope that your present sufferings are not the final cries in an empty universe. Instead, your cries are the prelude of joy at the final redemption. Through Christ, God has secured your eternal life and salvation. Because of that you can have hope; God is not done with you" (*Rid of My Disgrace*, 151).
5. U2, "Yahweh," *How to Dismantle an Atomic Bomb* © 2004 Island).
6. Mother Teresa, quoted in Ron Rhodes, *The Wonder of Heaven* (Eugene, OR: Harvest House, 2009), 203.
7. Peter Kreeft, *Heaven: The Heart's Deepest Longing* (San Francisco: Ignatius Press, 1989), 183.

CONCLUSION

If you've taken an art history class, you've probably come across Matthias Grünewald's *Isenheim Altarpiece*. Or at least the panel depicting the crucifixion. Completed in 1515, just before the Protestant Reformation blasted off, the altarpiece was commissioned for the church hospital of St. Anthony in Colmar, France, which specialized in comforting those dying with skin diseases. Grünewald took a radical approach to his subject. While most of his contemporaries were still depicting Calvary with post-Renaissance delicacy, Grünewald's version was dark and borderline horrific: especially Christ's smashed feet, His contorted arms, and His twisted hands. The cross is bowed to demonstrate Jesus bearing the sins of the world. The most shocking part of the piece, however, is that Jesus Himself has a skin disease; His loincloth is the same as the wrappings worn by the hospital's patients. The altarpiece is a creation of such shocking intensity that many initially—and even today—found it repulsive. Yet the graphic nature served masterfully to define and illustrate the Antonite brothers' powerful understanding of Christian ministry. Apparently patients were brought before the piece in order to meditate on it as they died. The brothers were a quiet order, so no explanations were provided. There was no awkward chatter, no halfhearted attempts to piously let God off the hook. There was just silence.

We have spoken at great length in this book about the approach embodied by those monks, what we have come to know as the theology of the cross. The theology of the cross does not invite those who are suffering to ponder the hidden things of God. "Why me?" Instead, one is brought face-to-face with the Suffering Servant Himself. This is opposed to what we've described as a "theology of glory," which holds that we can invite Jesus and His cross to be a part of our lives, a means to an end as opposed to the end itself. Instead of being brought forward to die well, we piously spend all of our time trying to improve ourselves "every day, in every way."

In practice, the theology of the cross understands the gospel as the entirety of Christian ministry. We never move beyond our need for a savior—indeed, our need for conversion—and any "good" that does take place is the fruit of faith in Christ. We come to God on our knees and with heavy hearts—but we find to our surprise (grace is always a surprise!) that we are met not with advice or platitudes about growth, but with absolution and mercy. One hundred percent. With renewed faith in the grace of God found in the crucified Christ, we might even find ourselves moving out into the world with a bit more freedom from the ever-shifting laws we place ourselves under. Indeed, with a bit more freedom from ourselves.

There's no doubt, the Why questions of suffering are utterly perplexing. And as we search the Scriptures and consider stories such as Job's, we are tempted to see those as worst-case scenarios designed to help us get our heads straight in relation to our comparatively small "first world" problems. We look for ways to manage pain. We medicate; we minimize; we moralize. We rage, and we run. We develop theories to explain what is happening to us. While they may temporarily help us categorize and compartmentalize our thoughts and feelings, when true suffering comes, all our speculations fall flat. The Whys of suffering keep us shrouded in a seemingly bottomless void of abstraction where God is reduced to a finite ethical agent, a limited psychological personality, whose purposes measure on the same scale as ours. But since no one alive can see the beginning from the end, from the divine vantage point, we're left stranded in a prison of inscrutability.[1] And sadly, we often prefer our confinement to the disorienting possibility that our suffering is actually ordained, that God is involved in it. Ray Ortlund said this: "When the righteous cannot connect the realities of their experience with the truths of God, then God is calling them to trust him that there is more to it than they can see. As with Job, there is a battle being fought in the heavenlies. Trust in God, not explanations from God, is the pathway through suffering."[2]

Fortunately, we worship a God who is in the business of freeing captives and creating trust where there was none before. In fact, the cross tells us that He does so (and has done so) through suffering, not despite it.

> Grace is available because Jesus went through the valley of the shadow of death and rose from death. The gospel engages our life with all its pain, shame, rejection, lostness, sin, and death. So now, to your pain, the gospel says, "You will be healed." To your shame, the gospel says, "You can now come to God in confidence." To your rejection, the gospel says, "You are accepted!" To your lostness, the gospel says, "You are found and I won't ever let you go." To your sin, the gospel says, "You are forgiven and God declares you pure and righteous." To your death, the gospel says, "You once were dead, but now you are alive."[3]

And let us not forget our friend Job, who was refused his Why so that he might recognize the Who. Oddly enough, even Job's story testifies to the truth of that blessed little formula: *Jesus plus nothing equals everything*. Our hope is not Jesus plus an explanation as to why suffering happens or Jesus plus an explanation as to why your child or spouse is so difficult, why the cancer hasn't gone into remission, why finances continue to be so tight.

Thomas Merton once said, "The truth that many people don't understand, until it is too late, is that the more you try to avoid suffering, the more you suffer, because smaller and more insignificant things begin to torture you in proportion to your fear of being hurt."[4] Think about it for a moment: What is that thing in your life that if God were to take it away, you'd feel like life was not worth living? When we're able to answer that question, we will figure out what we are really worshipping, and what, by definition, might lie at the root of our suffering. It could be our children, our spouse, an ambition, or a dream of financial success. Those good gifts God gave us for our enjoyment that we have turned into idols. Suffering is often the process of these things being stripped away. Indeed, there is nothing like suffering to remind us how much we need God. What good news that His purpose and plan for our lives moves in a different direction from ours!

The good news of suffering is that it brings us to the end of ourselves—a purpose it has certainly served in my life. It brings us to the place of honesty, which is the place of desperation, which is the place of faith, which is the place of freedom. Suffering leaves our idols in pieces on the ground. It puts us in a position to see that God sent His Son not only to suffer in our place but also to suffer with us. Our merciful friend has been through it all. He is with us right now! And while He may not deliver us from pain and loss, He'll walk with us through it. That is simply Who He is.

> For we do not have a high priest who is unable to sympathize with our weaknesses, but we have one who has been tempted in every way, just as we are—yet was without sin. Let us then approach

> the throne of grace with confidence, so that we may receive mercy and find grace to help us in our time of need. (Heb. 4:15–16)

After I preached the series on Job that this book is loosely based on, I heard from many of my congregants who had suffered in ways they could never have ever predicted. Their testimonies could be summed up like this: God has shown me who He is in brand-new ways, and now I'm able to say with Job: "Before my ears had heard of you, but now my eyes have seen you." They have experienced firsthand the reality that God-sent afflictions are often merciful intrusions designed to wake us up and break the chains of slavery to self-reliance. Indeed, their circumstances may not have changed, but their step is undeniably a bit lighter, their laugh a bit louder, their love a bit less self-conscious. Suffering makes us free.

And yet, our hope does not ultimately lie in our present liberation. There is no guarantee that we will experience relief from pain. I wish I could say there was. This life may feel like one long, painful death. All you can do is hang on, and sometimes you can't even do that. Fortunately, the good news of the gospel is not an admonition to hang on to God with all your strength and willpower and you'll be okay. The good news of the gospel is not some gnostic encouragement to view your suffering in the right way, or understand the theology of the cross more deeply. No, the good news is that God is hanging on to you. He's not waiting for you to save yourself or mature into someone who no longer needs Him. He will not let you go, come what may. Jesus will never, ever leave you or forsake you. Nothing you can do or not do can separate you from the love of Christ. In fact the only thing God needs from you is the only thing you may ultimately have to offer Him: your death. As Robert Farrar Capon said so beautifully:

> For Jesus came to raise the dead. He did not come to reward the rewardable, improve the improvable, or correct the correctable; he came simply to be the resurrection and the life of those who will take their stand on a death he can use instead of on a life he cannot.[5]

Perhaps you feel like a bereft patient sitting in a silent hospital, waiting for what comes next. Or maybe it's just that you can't seem to beat your depression, your addiction, or your anger. Or maybe you're terribly lonely, even in a crowded room. Maybe you've just had a really bad day. Regardless of what you are facing, know this: suffering is not final. Death is not the end. It wasn't for Jesus, and it's not for you. No amount of hurt or misfortune or ugliness can change that. This is why the apostle Paul was able to make such a gloriously absurd statement as "To live is Christ and to die is gain." In the light of the cross, suffering and death are more than inevitable; they are good.

Now that's what I call freedom. Indeed, that's what I call gospel-soaked liberation. Uncle!

NOTES

1. Hart commented on a famous article written by J. L. Makie from 1955 that argues that we must conclude from the evidences of history and nature that if God is indeed omnipotent, He manifestly is no good, and that if He is good, He manifestly is not omnipotent. Commenting on the article, Ron Rosenbaum wrote in the *New York Observer* that there is yet to be anyone to refute the Makie article. Here is Hart's response: "In point of fact, though, there is no argument here to refute; the entire case is premised upon an inane anthropomorphism—abstracted from any living system of belief—that reduces God to a finite ethical agent, a limited psychological personality, whose purposes are measurable upon the same scale as ours, and whose ultimate ends for his creatures do not transcend the cosmos as we perceive it. This is not to say that it is an argument without considerable emotional and even moral force; but of logical force there is none. Unless one can see the beginning and end of all things, unless one possesses a divine, eternal vantage upon all of time, unless one knows the precise nature of the relation between divine and created freedom, unless indeed one can fathom *infinite* wisdom, one can draw no conclusions from finite experience regarding the coincidence in God of omnipotence and perfect goodness. One may still hate God for worldly suffering, if one chooses, or deny him, but one cannot in this way 'disprove' him" (David Bentley

Hart, *The Doors of the Sea* [Grand Rapids, MI: Eerdmans, 2005], 13–14).

2. Ray Ortlund, "The Book of Job," Gospel Coalition, February 21, 2010, accessed June 6, 2012, http://thegospelcoalition.org/blogs/rayortlund/2010/02/21/the-book-of-job/.
3. Justin S. Holcomb and Lindsey A. Holcomb, *Rid of My Disgrace: Hope and Healing for Victims of Sexual Assault* (Wheaton, IL: Crossway, 2011), 208.
4. Thomas Merton, quoted in Charlette Mikula, *Peace in the Heart and Home* (Newton, NJ: Kittacanoe Press, 2001), 32.
5. Robert Farrar Capon, *Kingdom, Grace, Judgment* (Grand Rapids, MI: Eerdmans, 2002), 317.

BIBLIOGRAPHY

Allender, Dan B., and Tremper Longman III. *The Cry of the Soul: How Our Emotions Reveal Our Deepest Questions about God.* Colorado Springs, CO: NavPress, 1994.

Arendt, Hannah. *The Human Condition: A Study of the Central Dilemmas Facing Modern Man*. Garden City, NY: Doubleday, 1959.

Assayas, Michka, *Bono on Bono*. New York: Hodder & Stoughton, 2005.

Brown, Steve. *A Scandalous Freedom: The Radical Nature of the Gospel.* West Monroe, LA: Howard Books, 2004.

Capon, Robert Farrar. *Kingdom, Grace, Judgment: Paradox, Outrage, and Vindication in the Parables of Jesus*. Grand Rapids, MI: Eerdmans, 2002.

___________. *The Third Peacock*. San Francisco: Harper & Row, 1986.

Cary, Phillip. *Good News for Anxious Christians.* Grand Rapids, MI: Brazos Press, 2010.

Crabb, Larry. *Shattered Dreams: God's Unexpected Path to Joy.* Colorado Springs, CO: WaterBrook Press, 2001.

Dubus, Andre. *Broken Vessels.* Boston: David R. Godine, 1992.

Dumbrell, William J. *The Search for Order: Biblical Eschatology in Focus*. Eugene, OR: Wipf & Stock, 2001.

Eliot, T. S. *The Cocktail Party*. New York: Mariner Books, 1964.

Elliott, Matthew A. *Faithful Feelings: Rethinking Emotion in the New Testament*. Grand Rapids, MI: Kregel, 2006.

Eyer, Richard C. *Pastoral Care under the Cross*. St. Louis, MO: Concordia, 1995.

Forde, Gerhard O. *On Being a Theologian of the Cross*. Grand Rapids, MI: Eerdmans, 1997.

________. *Where God Meets Man*. Minneapolis: Augsburg Publishing House, 1972.

Hart, David Bentley. *The Doors of the Sea*. Grand Rapids, MI: Eerdmans, 2005.

Holcomb, Justin S. *On the Grace of God*. Wheaton, IL: Crossway, forthcoming.

Holcomb, Justin S., and Lindsey A. Holcomb. *Rid of My Disgrace: Hope and Healing for Victims of Sexual Assault*. Wheaton, IL: Crossway, 2011.

Horton, Michael. *A Place for Weakness*. Grand Rapids, MI: Zondervan, 2010.

Illouz, Eva. *Oprah Winfrey and the Glamour of Misery: An Essay on Popular Culture*. New York: Columbia University Press, 2003.

Jeffery, Steve, Michael Ovey, and Andrew Sach. *Pierced for Our Transgressions: Rediscovering the Glory of Penal Substitution*. Wheaton, IL: Crossway, 2007.

Johnson, Eric L. *Foundations of Soul Care: A Christian Psychology Proposal*. Downers Grove, IL: IVP Academic, 2007.

Keller, Timothy. *Counterfeit Gods: The Empty Promises of Money, Sex, and Power and the Only Hope that Matters*. New York: Dutton, 2009.

________. "The Gospel in All Its Forms." *Christianity Today*, May 2008.

________. "How Could a Good God Allow Suffering?" In *The Reason for God*. New York: Dutton, 2008, 22–34.

Kierkegaard, Søren. *A Kierkegaard Anthology*. Ed. Robert Bretall. Princeton, NJ: Princeton University Press, 1973.

Kreeft, Peter. *Heaven: The Heart's Deepest Longing*. San Francisco: Ignatius Press, 1989.

Lewis, C. S. *Mere Christianity*. New York: Macmillan, 1952.

________. *The Weight of Glory and Other Addresses*. Grand Rapids, MI: Eerdmans, 1965.

Lofton, Kathryn. *Oprah: The Gospel of an Icon*. University of California Press, 2011.

Luther, Martin. *Commentary on St. Paul's Epistle to the Galatians*. Trans. Theodore Conrad Graebner. Grand Rapids, MI: Zondervan, 1939.

________. *Day by Day We Magnify Thee: Daily Readings*. Philadelphia: Fortress, 1982.

________. *The Heidelberg Disputation*. http://www.academici.com/blog.aspx?bid=3373.

________. *Luther's Werke*. Weimar, 1883.

________. *Luther's Works*, Vol. 31, *Career of the Reformer*. Ed. Harold J. Grimm and Helmut T. Lehmann. Philadelphia: Fortress Press, 1957.

Lyons, William E. *Emotion*. Cambridge: Cambridge University Press, 1980.

Martyn, Dorothy. *Beyond Deserving: Children, Parents and Responsibility Revisited*. Grand Rapids, MI: Eerdmans, 2007.

McGrath, Alister E. *Luther's Theology of the Cross*. Malden, MA: Blackwell Publishing, 1985.

Morgan, Christopher W., and Robert A. Peterson, eds. *Suffering and the Goodness of God*. Wheaton, IL: Crossway, 2008.

Morris, Leon. *The Atonement: Its Meaning and Significance*. Downers Grove, IL: InterVarsity, 1983.

Murray, John. *The Atonement*. Philadelphia: P&R, 1962.

________. *Redemption Accomplished and Applied*. Grand Rapids, MI: Eerdmans, 1984.

O'Connor, Flannery. *Mystery and Manners: Occasional Prose*. New York: Farrar, Straus & Giroux, 1970.

Owen, John. *Overcoming Sin and Temptation*. Ed. Kelly M. Kapic and Justin Taylor. Wheaton, IL: Crossway, 2006.

Packer, J. I. *Knowing God*. Downers Grove, IL: InterVarsity, 1973.

Peterson, David. *Where Wrath and Mercy Meet: Proclaiming the Atonement Today*. Carlisle, UK: Paternoster, 2001.

Placher, William C. *The Domestication of Transcendence*. Louisville, KY: Westminster John Knox Press, 1996.

Plantinga, Cornelius. *Not the Way It's Supposed to Be: A Breviary of Sin*. Grand Rapids, MI: Eerdmans, 1995.

Powlison, David. *Seeing with New Eyes: Counseling and the Human Condition through the Lens of Scripture*. Phillipsburg, NJ: P&R, 2003.

________. *Speaking Truth in Love*. Greensboro, NC: New Growth Press, 2005.

Rhodes, Ron. *The Wonder of Heaven*. Eugene, OR: Harvest House, 2009.

Richardson, Ethan. *This American Gospel: Public Radio Parables and the Grace of God*. Charlottesville, VA: Mockingbird, 2012.

Scarry, Elaine. *The Body in Pain: The Making and Unmaking of the World*. New York: Oxford University Press, 1987.

Smedes, Lewis B. *Forgive and Forget: Healing the Hurts We Don't Deserve*. San Francisco: Harper & Row, 1984.

________. *Shame and Grace*. San Francisco: Harper San Francisco, 1993.

Sontag, Susan. *Regarding the Pain of Others*. New York: Farrar, Straus and Giroux, 2002.

Sproul, R. C. *Surprised by Suffering*. Wheaton, IL: Tyndale, 1988.

Stott, John R. W. *The Cross of Christ*. Downers Grove, IL: InterVarsity, 1986.

Volf, Miroslav. *End of Memory: Remembering Rightly in a Violent World*. Grand Rapids, MI: Eerdmans, 2006.

________. *Exclusion and Embrace: A Theological Exploration of Identity, Otherness, and Reconciliation*. Nashville: Abingdon, 1996.

________. *Free of Charge: Giving and Forgiving in a Culture Stripped of Grace*. Grand Rapids, MI: Zondervan, 2006.

Wilkerson, Mike. *Redemption: Freed by Jesus from the Idols We Worship and the Wounds We Carry*. Wheaton, IL: Crossway, 2011.

Wright, N. T. *Evil and the Justice of God*. Downers Grove, IL: InterVarsity, 2006.

Yancey, Phillip. *Disappointment with God*. Grand Rapids, MI: Zondervan, 1988.

Z., John. *Grace in Addiction: What Christians Can Learn From Alcoholics Anonymous.* Charlottesville, VA: Mockingbird, 2012.

Zahl, Paul F. M. *Grace in Practice: A Theology of Everyday Life.* Grand Rapids, MI: Eerdmans, 2007.

________. *The Merciful Impasse: The Sermon on the Mount for Those Who've Crashed (and Burned).* Charlottesville, VA: Mockingbird, 2011.

________. *Who Will Deliver Us? The Present Power of the Death of Christ.* Eugene, OR: Wipf & Stock, 2008.

FOR MORE BOOKS, SERMONS, VIDEOS, AND RESOURCES FROM TULLIAN TCHIVIDJIAN:

WWW.LIBERATENET.ORG
WWW.CRPC.ORG
@PASTORTULLIAN